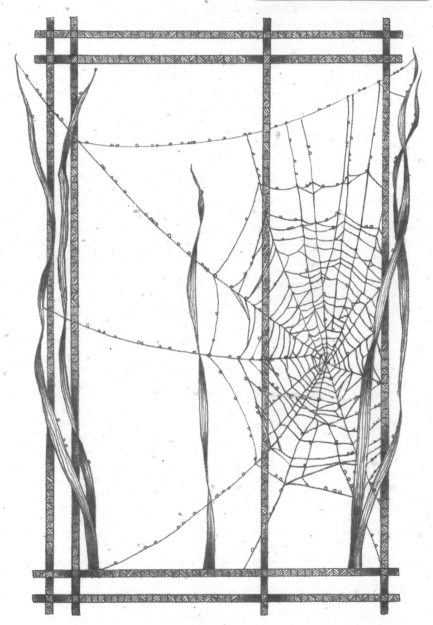

# Dewdrops on Spiderwebs

Nancy,
May writing be as
life-giving for you as it
has been for me!

*[signature]*

# Dewdrops on Spiderwebs

*Connections
Made
Visible*

## Susan Classen

HERALD PRESS
Scottdale, Pennsylvania
Waterloo, Ontario

**Library of Congress Cataloging-in-Publication Data**
Classen, Susan, 1957-
    Dewdrops on spiderwebs: connections made visible / Susan
Classen.
        p.   cm.
    Includes bibliographical references.
    ISBN 0-8361-9066-1 (alk. paper)
    1. Meditations.  2. Christianity—Central America.  3. Classen,
Susan, 1957-   . 4. Central America—Church history—
20th century.  I. Title.
BV4832.2.C538  1997
242—dc21                                                    96-52277

The paper used in this publication is recycled and meets the minimum
requirements of American National Standard for Information Sciences—
Permanence of Paper for Printed Library Materials, ANSI Z39.48-1984.

DEWDROPS ON SPIDERWEBS
Copyright © 1997 by Herald Press, Scottdale, Pa. 15683
Published simultaneously in Canada by Herald Press,
Waterloo, Ont. N2L 6H7. All rights reserved
Library of Congress Catalog Number: 96-52277
International Standard Book Number: 0-8361-9066-1
Printed in the United States of America
Book design by Gwen M. Stamm/Cover and inside art by Teresa
Pankratz

    05 04 03 02 01 00 99 98 97 10 9 8 7 6 5 4 3 2 1

*I* am the breeze that nurtures all things green.
*I encourage blossoms to flourish with ripening fruits.*
*I am the rain coming from the dew*
*that causes the grasses to laugh*
*with the joy of life.*

God speaks to Hildegard of Bingen,
eleventh century

# Contents

# Author's Preface

I'VE FELT CONNECTED to those of you now reading these essays since I began writing. Initially I felt bound as I struggled with the fear of making myself vulnerable to strangers and the pressure of meeting expectations. But I gradually let go of my fears and began to experience your presence in a life-giving way. As I wrote my thoughts and ideas, I found myself in dialogue with you, wondering what ideas you have on questions I deal with, wondering how the circumstances of your life have played out universal issues like letting go, surrendering control, and celebrating the wonder of God.

These essays resisted being rushed! I was excited about returning to Central America to begin a new Mennonite Central Committee term and wished I could put in long hours writing to finish quickly and be on my way. But I had to lay aside my agenda for the ideas to take visible form. I'm guessing that the same will be true for you as you read. You will need to read the essays one at a time without hurrying to finish the book.

I doubt that you will find many new insights in these reflections. Rather, you will find age-old insights as they work themselves out in one person's life—mine. They

will take root in you to the extent that you listen to the
Spirit moving in your own daily life.

I noticed as I wrote that several aspects of my life sto-
ry came up again and again. Let me mention them brief-
ly to provide context for my thoughts. After three years
in Bolivia and ten years in El Salvador with the Menno-
nite Central Committee (MCC), I decided to take a sab-
batical. I began with six months of solitude in rural Ken-
tucky. Then I studied for a term at a Mennonite semi-
nary before traveling in the United States for six months
to become reacquainted with my own country.

My mother died of cancer in 1981 and my father of a
brain tumor in 1990. Their life and death are insepara-
bly woven into my being. Ann Manganaro, a friend and
co-worker in El Salvador, also died of cancer in 1993.
She was a Sister of Loretto and a pediatrician. The fre-
quency with which I mention Mary Kennedy indicates
the depth to which our friendship has touched my life.
Mary is a Catholic sister with the School Sisters of Notre
Dame community. We lived together in El Salvador and
traveled together this summer.

The title, *Dewdrops on Spiderwebs: Connections Made
Visible*, was inspired by my experience with industrious
spiders in rural Kentucky.

The spiders around the cabin where I lived last sum-
mer were diligent. Every night they would spin their
webs and every day I would unwittingly walk into one
of their all-but-invisible traps, filling my hair with sticky
globs. But sometimes the early morning dew outlined
the intricate webs with delicate drops. The "traps" came
to life as elaborate works of art.

A smile came to my lips one morning as it occurred to me that the Holy Spirit is like the drops of dew on a spiderweb. The Spirit makes God visible in the ordinary, everyday aspects of life. The dew of the Spirit also makes our interconnectedness visible. God did not create us to be self-sufficient and autonomous but interdependent.

The writing process has been life-giving. I'm always amazed at the thoughts and feelings that surface when I allow the Spirit time and space! My prayer is that the Spirit will invite you to a deeper relationship with God, with yourself, and with others as you read.

—*Susan Classen*
  *Nicaragua*

# Dewdrops on Spiderwebs

# Beauty Draws Me Home

Beauty offers me glimpses of God's intentions in creating the world and hints of God's dreams for the future. I'm becoming aware that I've been more in touch with God's pain than with God's joy. Yet pain and joy are inseparably linked. When I allow myself to feel pain, I experience God's creative energy infusing life into suffering. I can point out the problems but I can't live out God's vision unless I allow beauty to draw me home to God's hopes and dreams.

# A Softened
# Heart

*A new heart I will give you, and a new spirit I will
put within you; and I will remove from your body
the heart of stone and give you a heart of flesh.*
—*Ezekiel 36:26*

ROSEL, A FRIEND of Mary's, is a talented musician who
studied Thomas Aquinas and put his thoughts to music.
I've never studied Thomas Aquinas but carry a stereo-
typical image of a cold and rational theologian. I was
delighted, then, to listen to Rosel's music and experi-
ence a different side of Aquinas. The composition, enti-
tled "Sheer Joy," provides clues for softening my "heart
of stone."

I hastily scribbled notes. Verse one describes Aquinas'
thought that "beauty is like a magnet that draws us
home." The second verse says love melts us. Verse three
says melting makes us ready to enjoy the Beloved. The
last verse proclaims that "joy expands the heart."

I think about this. Beauty draws me home to myself

and my Creator. The love I experience there melts my
defenses, softens my heart. Softening makes me recep-
tive to Christ, the Beloved. My softened heart expands
to hold the overflowing joy with which God longs to fill
me.

I've been attracted to "heart" images in recent years. I
was dealing with my father's death and the war in El Sal-
vador when a friend said I was sighing often. I realized
the sighs were an unconscious effort to loosen the band
of sorrow around my chest. I eventually learned to rec-
ognize the tightness in my chest as the Spirit's invitation
for me to look inward.

When dealing with Ann's death, I wrote in my journal, "Pain isn't neutral. It hardens or softens my heart."
I desperately hoped that the pain of loss would make
me more compassionate. But I was aware that for the
pain to soften my heart, I would have to stop resisting
it. Resisting pain, ignoring it, or plunging forward would
only harden my heart. Instead of having room for the
pain of others, I would tell people to deal with their
pain as I had mine—"Pull yourself together and get on
with it!"

A member of a delegation to El Salvador read my
book before she visited. After several days with me she
said she never would have guessed from my book that
I was so joyful! I had to laugh, particularly since others
have said the same. God used the writing to melt my de-
fenses, making me more receptive to the grace of Christ
offered through the Salvadoran people during the years
that followed. My heart has more room for joy now!

God doesn't chisel away the stone I carry in my heart.

Rather God gently invites me to receive the love that melts the pockets of resistance. Beauty and love soften my heart so it can expand to cradle both joy and pain.

The war in El Salvador and the death of people close to me revealed my resistance to pain. What pain have you experienced? How does the way you deal with your pain affect your response to others? What stones of resistance would God like to soften with love and beauty?

# Beauty and Pain

*It is powerless people . . . who can distance themselves from the human quest for security enough to open themselves to God's power.* —*Alan Kreider*

I FIND THAT SOME of the people society judges useless are the ones who most effectively reflect the beauty of God's desire for intimacy with us.

I learned yesterday that Choncito died. Choncito was from the village where I lived in El Salvador. He was learning disabled, hard of hearing, almost blind, and totally dependent on what others gave him to survive. But every Sunday he haltingly made his way up to the altar to deposit his coins in the offering plate. I remember thinking one Sunday morning that God must be very humble to receive an offering made with such sacrifice.

Another example comes to mind. At Ann's funeral, a friend shared an experience that took place while Ann was doing her residency in a neonatal intensive care unit.

There she cared for a five-inch premature baby named Tamika. She was left to die in the hospital with no love from her family. She smiled once, cupped in Ann's hands, after weeks of being held, caressed and gazed upon. Then she died.

After we two buried Tamika with the help of a generous funeral director, I protested to Ann that it all felt so meaningless and bleak. "What on earth did Tamika ever have?"

"Well," Ann said, "she had the power to evoke love from me."

And so it would be with Ann, just hours before she died, with all of her powers so diminished, her lively mind so quiet, her loving actions now gone. All that was left of Ann was what she shared with Tamika: the power to evoke our love. And God's.[1]

"People with power do not evoke intimacy," Henri Nouwen writes. "We fear people with power. . . . But God does not want us to be afraid, distant, or envious.

"God wants to come close, so that we can rest in the intimacy of God like children in their mothers' arms."[2]

God comes to us through powerlessness in order to invite us to a loving, intimate relationship. There is both pain and beauty in that relationship. Mary expressed the dilemma well in a tape she sent from Honduras.

It's a contradiction that as I experience the pain and see the tearful face of God suffering among us, I also look into God's eyes and see the beauty in the midst of suffering. That's where it's most difficult for me to find beauty. So when I sing, "I walk with beauty all around me," I'm not just singing about the beauty of the Bay Islands or the beauty of a pine forest or full moon. But I'm standing in the midst of broken down houses and abused children and still singing, "I walk with beauty all around me. . . ." It's quite a challenge.

The circumstances of my life don't force me to recognize my powerlessness and vulnerability. Unlike poor people struggling on the edge of survival, I can create for myself illusions of control. Yet God invites me over and over to recognize my fundamental vulnerability and dependence. Last week's blizzard was one such invitation.

One of the biggest snowstorms of the century hit the U.S. East Coast several days before I was to fly to Baltimore. I left the first day the airport reopened. The plane ride seemed more like a Salvadoran bus than an American airplane. And it wasn't just because the plane was packed full. The buzz of conversation filled the plane during the entire two-hour trip. Strangers told each other their stories of being delayed by the snowstorm. People helped each other with their luggage and didn't complain about the crowded seats. The mood was jovial and friendly.

I have never experienced that kind of interaction among airline passengers. What made the difference? I think strangers treated each other as human beings because we all knew we were out of control. The storm reminded us of our vulnerability and need for one another. We couldn't maintain illusions of being independent or self-sufficient.

There is nothing beautiful about the accidents, delays,

and deaths caused by the blizzard. Nor is there beauty in the misery and suffering caused by injustice around the world. But painful circumstances make us transparent, revealing both the best and the worst in us.

If I want to experience the beauty of intimacy, I must allow my protective buffers to drop and accept my innate vulnerability. I wonder how you experience the contradiction of beauty in the midst of pain.

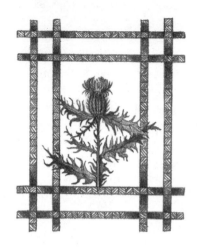

# Bonds, Not Chains

*. . . all my good friends around me and I felt a great bond with each one in a different way, a bond that was not a chain.* —*Etty Hillesum*

I SIT QUIETLY SIPPING a cup of coffee and musing over the past months. It has been almost four months since Mary began her trip by land back to Honduras and I boarded an airplane to continue my travels in the U.S. Even now a few tears slip down my cheeks.

It's difficult to describe how I feel. I'm aware of sadness. Yet at the same time my heart sings with gratitude for the beauty of friendship. As Mary said reflectively one evening, "How deeply I feel the pain is how deeply I've felt the joy."

I think about the relationship between pain and joy. If there is no room for suffering in my life there is no room for joy. A mental picture comes to mind.

The Salvadoran peasants knew every nook and cranny in the hillsides around our village. They knew every tree, every swimming hole, every pure mountain spring. I would look at the natural basin of rocks that they pointed out as a spring and see muck, sticks, and leaves. But the Salvadorans would scoop out the water and clean out the leaves and mud. Then the pure spring water would slowly seep from the rocks and fill the basin. The freshness of joy can only seep into my character where pain has cleared a space in my heart.

As I write this morning, I'm struck with the lessons of life presented to me through my friendship with Mary. The relationship between pain and joy is one. Learning to let go is another.

Perhaps the bond between Mary and me grew so strong because it was clear from the beginning that our friendship was a gift of God's grace. Mary is a Catholic sister from Illinois who was working in Honduras and I a Mennonite nurse from Ohio working in El Salvador. A mutual friend brought us together when we happened to be visiting Kentucky at the same time. As a result, we lived and worked together for three years in El Salvador.

God's gifts can't be hoarded. I have to let go to receive God's provision one day at a time. As a single woman it's easy for me to romanticize marriage. "How nice it must be," I dream, "not to have to say good-bye to your spouse, to know your life calling is to be together." But I know deep down that letting go is essential to any healthy relationship. We all need the security of love without chains of neediness that control us.

I must allow myself to grieve, not only Mary's leaving but also the fact that we won't live together again in the foreseeable future. I can't welcome the new life that will come unless I let go of the past. As Mary expressed so well, "Part of my peace in living fully this pain is knowing that if we don't move through this stage we can't move on to the gift of the next moment God waits eagerly to give us."

I also learn about loneliness through my friends. Sometimes when I feel lonely I blame my friends for not adequately meeting my needs. It's also tempting to think that if I were married I wouldn't feel lonely. But I'm grateful when God's grace reveals my loneliness for what it really is—God's invitation to relationship.

It comes as no surprise, then, when my happily married friends tell me that they, too, struggle with loneliness. God plants in us a longing for relationship only God can fill. No committed friend, no loving spouse can ultimately fulfill the yearning of my heart. Loving my family and friends expands my heart to make more room for God. That is the beauty of friendship.

I've experienced the beauty of friendship through my relationship with Mary and other committed friends. But close friendships also reveal my loneliness. It's a challenge to let go and trust that God will meet my needs. What have you learned about yourself and God through significant relationships?

# Weeds

*But God chose what is foolish in the world to shame the wise; God chose what is weak in the world to shame the strong; God chose what is low and despised in the world, things that are not, to reduce to nothing things that are. —1 Corinthians 1:27-28*

CHARLES AND MOLLY inspire me through their appreciation of beauty. They are siblings, probably in their mid-fifties. They are learning disabled and care for their mother, herself severely disabled. But the state took custody of their mother until they could meet standards.

Charles was hot and sweaty when Rita, a public health nurse, and I arrived. He was busy working outside trying to clean up the junk surrounding the house. I looked around. Broken glass, a rusty washing machine, piles of old tires, and boxes of junk littered the yard. Animals roamed freely in and out of the house which had no running water or plumbing.

But their flower garden caught my eye. I like flowers,

so I asked about their garden. Pointing out one of their special flowers, they invited me to touch the soft bristles.

"It's like a powder puff," Charlie said grinning.

"I like the light purplish color," Molly added.

I stood in amazement, humbled by their appreciation of beauty. The flower was a thistle.

"We saw these growing last year in a ditch," Molly continued. "So we waited until the flowers dried, then we gathered the seeds and planted them here."

She offered to send me seeds when this year's blossoms dried. My amazement grew. Surely God "chose what is foolish in the world to shame the wise . . . God chose what is low and despised" (1 Cor. 1:27-28). Who says thistles are weeds?

The experience with Molly and Charles makes me think about more than appreciation of nature. What personal characteristics have I defined as thistles to be uprooted rather than flowers to be enjoyed?

In El Salvador I struggled with needing solitude in a culture where being alone is seen as a hardship. When my neighbors knew I was alone in the house, they would sometimes send their children over so I wouldn't be sad and lonely! I would get frustrated with myself when my need for quiet interfered with my ability to be hospitable to the visitors who frequently stopped by our house. Why couldn't I be more extroverted and spontaneous?

I've slowly come to see that my gifts lie in my need for solitude. Periods of quiet help me pray, write, reflect. Solitude frees the gifts I have to share. My desire for solitude isn't a thistle to uproot but a flower to appreciate. I know I'm not alone in sometimes feeling dissatisfied with myself. Perhaps you will find it helpful, as I have, to look for beauty in what you've defined as thistles. How do those characteristics reflect your gifts?

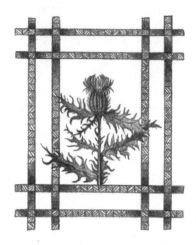

# Life-Giving Attitudes

*Finally, beloved, whatever is true, whatever is*
*honorable, whatever is just, whatever is pure,*
*whatever is pleasing, whatever is commendable,*
*if there is any excellence and if there is anything wor-*
*thy of praise, think about these things.*
*—Philippians 4:8*

THIS MORNING I'm thinking about three examples of attitudes that draw me home to God's vision for human relationships.

I met Cristina at a small group Bible study in Chicago. She is originally from Honduras but has lived the past number of years in the U.S. Cristina gave thanks to God for her twelve-year-old son's generosity.

Her son has a job selling candy and decided to buy a pair of name-brand tennis shoes. But once in the store he realized he didn't have enough money to buy the shoes he wanted and still buy a pair for his sister. He bought two pairs of cheaper shoes instead. He also gave Cristina $50 to send to his grandma in Honduras.

The beauty of his thoughtfulness makes God's dream visible. God created the world with the intention that everyone would have enough. Glimpses of that original vision inspire me along the way. The beauty is all the more compelling because self-centered values are often the norm and peer pressure frequently wins.

Another example comes to mind. Bill is an O'Odham Indian and a talented lay leader in the Catholic church. Alcoholism is a serious problem on the reservation and Bill, like many others, struggles daily with the temptation to drink. Bill laid open his soul at a gathering of O'Odham Christians. He shared that about once a year he has a relapse and drinks again. Overcome with guilt and shame, he withdraws from church involvement. But shame doesn't have the last word. His voice choked with emotion, Bill said, "I fail but get back up again and continue the journey."

The beauty of vulnerability is not only overlooked but often looked down on in a world that values strength, control, and success. Yet Bill makes God's dream of humble leaders visible. God needs leaders who know their dependence on God and use their own shortcomings to provide examples of humble perseverance.

Different cultures display God's beauty because each uniquely highlights some aspect of God's character. The beauty of God's friendliness shone through a stranger in rural West Virginia.

As I walked along a gravel road, I was struck by the fact that passing motorists almost invariably waved.

Then I noticed an inviting dirt road leading toward a cemetery and decided to explore. There was a closed gate across the road but I didn't notice any "No trespassing" signs, so I walked through. When I heard a truck behind me, though, I immediately wondered if an angry property owner was going to demand that I leave. Sure enough, the truck stopped beside me. I turned and was surprised to see a smiling driver. He said that he just couldn't pass by without stopping to say hello. He drove off leaving me touched by the glimpse of a world free of hostility and suspicion.

I feel challenged to be more attentive to beauty. Noticing beauty doesn't mean overlooking ugliness. Beautiful attitudes are made that much more compelling because they contrast with the fear and self-centeredness that govern many of our actions. They draw me home to the dream God plants within each one of us—a dream made visible by generosity, vulnerability, and trust.

Once I began reflecting on the beauty of life-giving attitudes I thought of one example after another. I wonder what examples you notice in your daily interaction with people. How are you affected by thinking about "whatever is true, whatever is honorable, just, pure, and pleasing"?

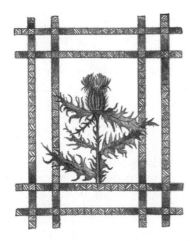

# "Trashing"
# My Values

*The heavens are telling the glory of God;*
*and the firmament proclaims his handiwork.*
*—Psalm 19:1*

GOD DRAWS ME home through the beauty of nature. But an incident at the Grand Canyon left me wondering if there are ways I unconsciously "trash" the beauty I value.

Mary and I spent several days at the Grand Canyon this summer. We got up at 4:30 a.m. one morning to watch the sun rise. Then we walked about nine miles along the rim of the canyon. We were pleased that we didn't see one tourist bus or other people until almost finished with our hike. It was as if God had given us the canyon to ourselves for several hours just to enjoy our delight!

We took a sightseeing bus back to the starting point, and I observed our fellow passengers. A family with three young children called my attention. The parents were calm and loving as they dealt with their lively youngsters and talked to them about the beauty of the canyon. I heard them tell another passenger they had driven from Oregon to Texas to visit friends and were now on their way home. I was impressed by the respect with which they treated each other and their children.

We arrived at our destination and found our car. I smiled when I noticed that the young family was in the car ahead of us. But my smile quickly faded when I saw a dirty disposable diaper fly out their window landing in the ditch! How could they! How could anyone experience the grandeur of God's creation, then trash it?

I have to smile even as I write because I was so upset by the incident. The fact that it stays with me means there must be something for me to learn. How do I "trash" the beauty I value?

I know I'm frequently unconscious of the beauty around me. When my mind is busy and distracted, I miss God's invitation through a flower, the sky, a budding tree. When pushing myself toward a goal or deadline, I'm so consumed I don't notice the beauty of my surroundings. When fearful or worried, I'm too focused on myself to be aware of God's subtle invitations.

I did allow nature to draw me home to God this fall in southern Michigan, however, and the experience was life-giving. One cloudy morning I felt so connected to the vibrant life pulsing through my surroundings that even inanimate objects seemed to take on a life of their own. I recorded my thoughts in my journal.

The beauty as I walked was compelling; not sunny or bright but compelling nonetheless. It was a foggy, damp day. Listening, I heard the dampness gather as drops and fall to the ground. Every leaf and weed shimmered. I was heading back to my room when an empty bench invited me. "No, I just washed my shoes and I would have to walk through the wet grass to get to you. . . . Well, okay. I'll walk carefully." I tiptoed to the bench and sat quietly— listening, being. After a few minutes I walked to the car to get something, again on my way to my room. I glanced across the field. The orange hue of changing leaves beckoned. "Come and see." "No, I can't. Sorry. The grass is too tall. I'll get my shoes and pants soaking wet." I climbed in the van and the next thing I knew I was putting on my old tennis shoes. So much for practicality. My shoes would dry and I could wash my clothes. I started down the path mowed through the hay field but the tree that called me wasn't on the path. I didn't even care anymore. I made my way through the field and greeted the tree. By this time I had my camera with me. Everything I saw was pure beauty.

I just looked out my window. A brightly decked blue jay is chirping enthusiastically. The winter sky is crisp and clear after days of rain; the ground is sprinkled with white powder. I think I'll go for a walk. Will you join me? We could talk about whether or not you "trash" your values and ways you are attentive to beauty.

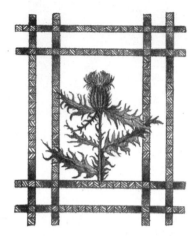

# A Green
# Leaf

*"Truly I tell you, unless you change and become like children, you will never enter the kingdom of heaven." —Mt. 18:3*

YOUNG CHILDREN are experts on awareness. They observe the smallest details and have a tremendous capacity to celebrate what I take for granted. A friend told a story about her young niece whose school class went on a field trip in the fall.

The students collected leaves on the trip and her niece was delighted to show her aunt her collection. "Look!" she exclaimed. "This leaf is orange. This one is orange and green. And look at this one," she added excitedly, "It's all green!"

When a green leaf calls forth awe and wonder, then all life is budding with reasons to celebrate! Children can teach me to appreciate what I take for granted, but all too often I'm not open to their wisdom. I don't recognize the opportunity to learn from them; I squelch their

God-given wonder with my superiority. "All leaves are green," I'm apt to respond in verbal or nonverbal ways. "Green leaves are nothing to get excited about." A characteristic I appreciated about the Salvadorans with whom I lived and worked was their childlike simplicity. One Christmas day, Mary and I brought out a bottle of bubbles. I'm not sure who enjoyed them more, three-year-old Carmen or her mother! It was delightful to experience their amazement and my own childlike spirit danced gratefully at the unexpected chance to play.

But North American cultural influences seem to strip children early of their innocence, delight, and wonder. A friend shared her concern about her nine-year-old daughter, who already stands in front of the mirror primping and talking about dates. "Where does that influence come from?" she asked in anguish. "We don't even have a TV."

Children in poor countries are robbed of their childhood because they have to work to survive. Children in North America are robbed of their childhood by a society that doesn't value their innate simplicity. Advertising tries to define our needs and promises to fulfill them. We are left searching endlessly for the contentment promised by products that are bigger, better, and more entertaining.

I stopped writing for a while and went out to rake leaves. I wondered as I raked if "ordinary" has negative connotations in North America. Have we become addicted to the thrill of the "extraordinary"?

What do you think?

# Quiet
# Space

*For thus said the Lord God, the Holy One of Israel:*
*In returning and rest you shall be saved; in quietness*
*and in trust shall be your strength. But you refused.*
*—Isaiah 30:15*

I SPENT SEVERAL WEEKS visiting the O'Odham Indian reservation in the Arizona desert. O'Odham means "Desert People." The beauty of the desert and people touched me.

Each morning I would sit outside enjoying the cool air and letting the vast desert envelop me. The silence was stunningly framed into quiet spaces by singing birds. I could see a few houses from the backyard but heard no sound. What a contrast to a Salvadoran village, where anyone who could afford batteries turned the radio on by 5:00 a.m. loud enough for family and neighbors to enjoy!

On our way to a public gathering, Janice, who lives and works on the reservation, assured us there was no need to make conversation. "The O'Odham are comfortable with silence," she explained. "As we eat together they may or may not talk."

Janice was right. There was little conversation. But the atmosphere was comfortable, inviting. I felt welcomed and embraced. There was no need to fill the empty spaces with words, no stilted effort to make small talk. Even the children played quietly. Only the crunch of gravel under bicycle wheels told me they were outside our house. Sometimes in the evening the youth played basketball on the nearby court. The dribbling ball and an occasional comment were all I heard.

Quiet. Even as I write I find my thoughts relaxing. There is no need to push the words or rush the process. Quiet. The frenetic energy built up inside slows.

After six months of traveling in the U.S., I was ready to settle in one place for several months. It was a relief to arrive at Cedars of Peace. In a letter to Mary I wrote gratefully, "The quiet here seeps into my soul."

"I dare say it isn't that the quiet 'seeps into your soul,' " she wisely said, "but that the quiet finally has a chance to seep out of your soul into the rest of you."

I easily forget I carry quiet in my soul. When frazzled I think the problem is that I'm too busy and need a peaceful environment. I do need peace sometimes but not so that quiet can seep into my soul. I need it to remind me the Spirit of peace is already present. My frenzy doesn't "rob" me of inner quiet. Rather, I get so wound up I forget peace is there, patiently awaiting my recognition.

In Isaiah, God promises strength through quietness and trust. What a tragedy that the verse ends, "But you refused." Help me, O God, to receive your quiet strength.

When busy I have to take time to let my spinning thoughts slow down to receive the quiet God offers. How receptive are you to the quiet God longs to give? What environment helps the quiet "seep into your being"?

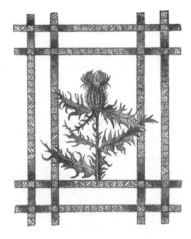

# Fulfilled or Filled Full?

*We had the experience but missed the meaning, and approach to the meaning restores the experience in a different form. . . — T. S. Eliot*

I ENJOY PLAYING with words and smiled ironically when the thought came to me that our desire for fulfilled lives often ends up in lives filled full. American life is full in many ways—full schedules, full shelves, full minds.

When Mary and I left El Salvador we traveled back to the U.S. by land. We made the trip by bus and train up through Mexico giving ourselves time to make a gradual transition. We were in Denver when I needed to buy some toothpaste. As I looked around the large discount store, I was impressed with the plastic storage boxes of every size and shape. Friends who know me well are no doubt smiling as they read this since they know I love boxes! I like being organized and having my things sorted and divided in boxes just the right size and shape.

I remembered the cardboard box under my bed in El

Salvador. It was a good box, the kind that holds canned milk. I probably got it easily from the local store because I was a foreigner. Others had to wait, because good boxes are valuable in Central America. I pictured having a plastic box under my bed. I wouldn't have to worry about contents getting damp on the dirt floor, and a tight lid would keep out roaches. But the longer I was in the U.S. the more I realized plastic boxes are everywhere!

Stores are full of products that make it convenient to keep clothes, tools, kitchen items. I noticed that even many small towns have long-term storage units for larger items. I'm told walk-in closets are standard in many new homes. Compared to my neighbors in El Salvador, my life is stuffed full of belongings. But is my life fulfilled?

Time is another crucial factor in our full lives. I remember when it struck me that we seemed to have developed a "planning ritual" on the MCC team. Whenever we needed to schedule a meeting we would all pull out our calendars, fretting and stewing about how busy we were. The unspoken assumption was that the best MCC-er was the one with the fullest calendar.

A friend wanted to invite me for a meal. He started out by going through his schedule for the week, explaining why he couldn't invite me on Monday, Tuesday, Wednesday. . . . Finally he got to Saturday and wondered if Saturday would suit.

I said yes, and we enjoyed a nice meal together. But I wondered why he felt he needed to explain his whole schedule. Why didn't he simply invite me for Saturday? Since then, I catch myself doing similar explaining. It's as if I have to prove I'm worthwhile by being busy. But a full schedule doesn't make a fulfilled life.

Even the airwaves are full. A university professor commented that her school has been unable to install interactive video because the airwaves are filled by radio stations, TV stations, and mobile phones.

I struggle for words to describe the need I sense for empty space. "Emptiness" can have negative connotations. If I say "I feel empty," I'm likely describing an uncomfortable feeling of being drained or vaguely depressed. Maybe that's why empty space in my life is crucial for feeling fulfilled. The emptiness provides a crack for God to work through. God doesn't need much. Just a crack in my full life is enough for the Spirit to begin nudging open a little more space in my heart.

As the Spirit stretches my heart, I begin to realize the emptiness isn't a void or a vacuum. Caryll Houselander uses the examples of a chalice, a reed, and a nest to describe emptiness with a purpose. A chalice is empty to be filled with wine. A reed channels the piper's breath into music. A nest provides a home for the young. I experience fulfillment as I allow God to fill my emptiness.

I'm challenged by the words of T. S. Eliot, "We had the experience but missed the meaning." It's hard to accept that I can't do it all, that I can't fill my life full of experiences and still have time to find the meaning in them. To allow room for empty space, I must resist my tendency to fill my life full. Emotion wells up as I write. Emptiness gives space to the yearning which lies dormant and neglected—a yearning God places within every person, a yearning only God can fulfill.

I wonder what connotations "emptiness" holds for you. Do you also tend to fill your life full, telling yourself someday, when you have time, you will process your experiences more fully? What are you learning as you search for fulfillment?

# The Better Part

*But the Lord answered her, "Martha, Martha, you are worried and distracted by many things; there is need of only one thing. Mary has chosen the better part, which will not be taken away from her."*
*—Luke 10:41-42*

I TOUCH THE BEAUTY of both faith and action as I realize they are one. I used to wonder how I could better integrate them. But it's futile to try to integrate two aspects that aren't divided! I can only ask God to help me see past the divisions that have been imposed so I can experience the fundamental unity of faith and action.

I remember sitting on the floor with a small group of women discussing Jesus' response to Mary and Martha. Martha was busy working while Mary sat quietly at Jesus' feet. Jesus tells Martha, "Mary has chosen the better part, which will not be taken away from her" (Luke 10:42). Does that mean that contemplative sitting is better than active working?

As we discussed the story, we reached the conclusion that Jesus wasn't referring to the fact that Martha was working and Mary sitting. Rather, he was responding to the inner attitude of the two women. Martha was frenzied and resentful, while Mary was quiet and peaceful. I can be running errands and carry Mary's peaceful spirit in me. Or my body can be sitting while my mind continues its frenzied pace. Just the other night, during community evening prayer, I sat quietly as usual while my mind was distracted by how I was going to fix the porch step the next day!

There are six cabins where I'm staying. Yesterday a woman left after being here three months. She was concerned about leaving this peace, wondering what will happen to her sense of tranquillity when she returns to her normal activities. Last year I was here for six months and wondered the same. It was reassuring to realize that the quiet, contemplative spirit Jesus called "the better part" doesn't depend on my physical surroundings.

I appreciate the emphasis the Quaker tradition places on silence. William Penn wrote in 1699, "True silence is the rest of the mind; and is to the spirit, what sleep is to the body, nourishment and refreshment." I need moments of silence to remind myself that faith and action are one.

To quiet my busy mind, I start the day by lighting a candle and sitting in silence for as long as it takes to drink a cup of coffee. The silence stills my soul so my mind and heart are quiet later when I bring specific people and events before God. I also find that repetitive movement, like walking, or an absorbing task with my hands, like needlework, helps quiet my mind. I wonder what you do to quiet your mind and heart. How does silence nurture your spirit?

# Freedom Through Surrender

I find myself uncomfortable writing about surrender. It's a concept that has been misused to promote passivity in the face of injustice. But I have to write about it because the Spirit is urging me to let go of control. I finally arrive at a simple but crucial truth: God doesn't invite me to surrender to suffering but to love.

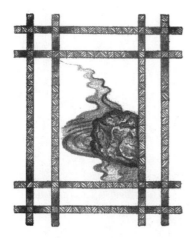

# Rocks Not Sponges

*But the wisdom from above is first pure, then peace-able, gentle, willing to yield, full of mercy and good fruits, without a trace of partiality or hypocrisy. And a harvest of righteousness is sown in peace for those who make peace. —James 3:17-18*

THE SPIRIT is inviting me to surrender. The invitation is open-ended and comes to me again and again in a variety of ways. I have to chuckle as I think of how I wish I could control the surrendering process! If only I could do it once and for all!

The current invitation involves letting go of the security and control provided by my intellect. There is nothing wrong with using my intellect. It's a gift from God. Perhaps it's so hard to surrender control precisely because it's one of my greatest gifts.

I remind myself that I'm surrendering to God. I'm surrendering to love, to the God of love, to the God who longs to breathe the breath of life into dry bones. I'm particularly sensitive to the need to be clear that I'm surrendering to the God of love because the biblical concept of surrender has often been misused.

I remember listening to a street evangelist preaching to a group of poor people in El Salvador. His text was Luke's story of the rich man and Lazarus. The preacher emphasized that Lazarus suffered patiently day after day as he begged by the gate and therefore received his reward in heaven. Linking Lazarus to the crowd listening to him, the evangelist explained that they, too, must accept their earthly suffering to receive their heavenly reward.

On another occasion, I was talking to a refugee about the unfair wage he received for the hammocks he made. I began to express an idea I thought would help improve his situation.

But he stopped me in mid-sentence. "I'm poor because God is punishing me," he said, ending the conversation. He thought trying to improve his life was to resist God's will to punish him.

Yielding to a God of love enables people creatively to stand against the powers that oppress them. But those in power have turned the tables on surrender. They teach the poor a theology that encourages them to surrender not to a God of love but to passivity and misery.

For years I've been intrigued by Vernard Eller's image of peacemakers as "rocks in a whirlpool." Only a firm rock can break the spin of whirling water. Peacemakers are called to be a firm, loving presence which breaks the spiral of escalating violence.

I've been moved by the stories of battered women in

North America and angered by the kind of theology that teaches women in abusive situations that love and for-giveness means submitting to violence. Too many wom-en are taught to be sponges that absorb violence rather than rocks that break the cycle. The longer a woman stays in an abusive situation, the more she absorbs the violence into herself until she believes she provokes the attacks and deserves to be beaten.

I pray, O God, for the wisdom to distinguish between dispelling violence and absorbing it into myself. May my life sow seeds of peace.

I wish I could hear what you have been taught about surrender and what it means to you now. How do you understand the difference between dispelling and ab-sorbing violence?

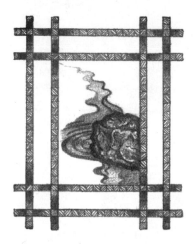

# The Cutting Edge

*Yield yourselves to the Lord and come to his
sanctuary. . . . For the Lord your God is gracious
and merciful, and will not turn away his face from
you, if you return to him.* —2 Chronicles 30:8-9

SURRENDER WAS A KEY concept to the Anabaptists. In Mennonite writings it is still often referred to as the German word *gelassenheit*. Gelassenheit has to do with a spirit of self-denial, surrender, openness to the will of God, readiness to suffer for God.

Yielding to God affected the daily lives of the Anabaptists. Gelassenheit was the basis for several important practices, including using their material possessions for the common good, refusing to defend themselves with the sword, and committing themselves to the discipline of the church body.

Robert Cornwall proposes that "self-denial and surrender to the will of God (gelassenheit) were at the center of the Anabaptist theology of suffering and martyrdom."³ Were they passively surrendering to oppressive powers? Does a theology of "gelassenheit" work against those on the bottom and in favor of those on top? I searched the historical texts for clues and was thrilled the day I found my answer. Alan Kreider researched the use of Scripture in the accounts preserved in the *Martyrs Mirror.* The most frequently cited Old Testament passage was Isaiah 49:15, "Can a woman forget her nursing child, or show no compassion for the child of her womb? Even these may forget, yet I will not forget you." The Anabaptists weren't surrendering to their persecutors but to the God of love and mercy.

My arms prickle with goose bumps as I write. Surrender to transforming love resulted in persecution and death. From the perspective of distance and security, we analyze the choices the Anabaptists made. The questions raised in an Anabaptist history class I took indicate our current mind-set. "How could they leave their families? Was it responsible for Anabaptist parents to make choices knowing their children could be left orphaned? Were the martyrs brainwashed?"

I wrote down a comment by the professor during our class discussion. "Little in [current] Mennonite church life conceives of making drastic decisions." The Anabaptists and many people currently experiencing persecution all over the world are faced with drastic situations that demand drastic responses. Our forebears were persecuted and killed for their faith. Generations of Mennonites following them have remembered and respected their choices.

But what about today? Can we conceive of making a

choice that demands our life? Are we so distant from the
need to take a stand for our faith that we now look back
on our heritage of suffering and wonder if the Anabap-
tists were crazy?

It's a disturbing thought. But I return to love. "Surren-
der to transforming love resulted in persecution and
death." No wonder I sometimes resist that love. The im-
plications are life-changing not just for the Anabaptist
martyrs but for me. Yielding myself to God's love isn't
pious spirituality removed from consequences in the
"real world." Receiving God's gracious love and mercy
puts me on the cutting edge of life.

I was excited when I realized that surrendering to
God isn't passive but active. What do you think about
the idea that yielding to God puts us on the cutting edge
of life? How does surrendering to the God of love affect
your response to injustice and oppression?

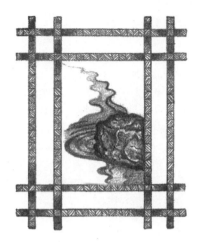

# Nothing Left to Blame

*Trust in the Lord, and do good; so you will live*
*in the land, and enjoy security. Take delight in the*
*Lord, and he will give you the desires of your heart.*
*—Psalm 37:3-4*

I KEEP THINKING about control issues in my life. Why is it so hard to trust that God will provide?

I remember times in El Salvador when my life was in danger from the fighting, when I was blacklisted by the army, when I was arrested. The stress and pressure were intense. I remember feeling angry, helpless, and frustrated—but I don't remember feeling stripped of control like I do now.

I wonder why. Perhaps it's because in El Salvador I always had someone to blame for making me feel powerless. It was the fault of the war, the army, the government, politics. . . .

An example of blaming comes to mind. We were trying to build latrines in the isolated village where I lived, but the army refused us permission to take in the materials we needed. The health workers and I blamed the army for our not having adequate latrines.

But after a number of months, the army finally gave us permission to take in the materials. The trucks came and we unloaded the supplies beside the church where they sat for months. Why? Because the fundamental problem wasn't the army; it was that people weren't convinced they needed latrines.

I feel stripped of control this week because I have no one and nothing left to blame. I have to deal with my own fundamental need to surrender and depend on God. I'm in a quiet, prayerful environment and have as much time as I need as I begin writing. There are no external factors I can blame for impeding the process.

Only the Spirit can unravel the issues. I can't study or research the topics because devotional reflection can only flow out of my own experience. I'm down to the bare bones choice of either depending totally on the Spirit or not writing this book.

I read Psalm 37 again. "Trust in the Lord, and do good; so you will live in the land, and enjoy security. Take delight in the Lord, and he will give you the desires of your heart." God doesn't ask me to live a precarious, insecure existence but to place my security in God rather than in my own abilities or possessions. Trusting in God's security purifies the desires of my heart so I can genuinely delight in the Lord.

I'm guessing that you also deal with control issues. I wonder what they are. What is the Spirit inviting you to surrender to experience God's security?

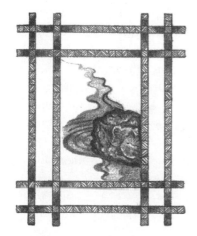

# Willpower
# and
# Surrender

*Mastery must yield to mystery.* —*Gerald May*

WHENEVER SOMEONE implies that I'm stubborn, I laugh and explain that I prefer to think of myself as "determined." I've been clearly influenced by the mind-set that says I can do anything if I try hard enough. I've had to think deeply, then, about my characteristic determination and how that gift can be surrendered to God.

Gerald May, in his book *Will and Spirit*, warns of the danger of assuming that we can master our destiny through willpower alone. He writes, "As a society, we are convinced that if we can only learn enough, become strong enough, and work hard enough, we can impose peace and fulfillment upon ourselves and everyone else. But the actual condition of the world and of our own hearts refutes this."[4] May concludes that we must learn to listen to the innate wisdom of our spirits, a wisdom that longs to surrender to life as mystery rather than a challenge to be conquered.

I remember a dream I had the first night after I was released from two days in a Salvadoran prison. I saw myself on a bicycle trying to force myself up a hill in the highest gear possible. It was clear that if I was going to last over the long haul I needed to learn to gear down and enjoy life instead of gutting it out to the top with determination and willpower.

I've accomplished a great deal through determination and willpower but in one key area—my tendency to get nervous in front of other people—willpower has failed every time.

Willpower has tried for years to tell me that I can control my shaking hands and voice if I just try hard enough. I'm not sure exactly when I started getting nervous but I have memories of piano contests and French horn performances in high school during which I shook like a leaf. I remember discovering that I didn't seem to get nervous speaking, just in performing music. But at some point I found myself struggling even with getting up and saying my name when visiting a new church.

It has been clear for some time that determination wasn't enough—but what to do? I wasn't aware of other ways of coping. Did accepting myself mean admitting I wasn't cut out for public speaking? Would it be best to stop trying since trying harder was making me worse?

Last year I was preparing for a speaking engagement and found myself uptight and nervous weeks ahead of time. I spent hours preparing so I could be sure every detail was covered. The more nervous I felt, the more I prepared. I thought if I could only make sure I was ready, then I would feel relaxed and secure!

A breakthrough came when I realized that I was depending on being prepared for my security rather than surrendering to the spontaneity of the Spirit. I threw away the talk I had carefully written out and used an outline instead. The outline evidently provided the needed opening for the Spirit because I was amazed when I heard the words flowing out of my mouth!

Although I'm always nervous before I speak, I'm learning to accept it as natural for me. On good days I'm even grateful because the jitters bring my energy to the surface, making it available for the Spirit to channel in constructive ways.

Instead of trying to conquer my problem through willpower, I'm learning to yield to the mystery of the power of grace. When I feel nervous I try to resist my natural impulse to keep my eyes glued to the words written on the paper in front of me and surrender to the Word within me.

I tend to depend on being prepared for my security rather than on the Spirit. What do you depend on for your security? How have you experienced the tension between trying hard and surrendering to God?

# And God Smiled

*My grace is sufficient for you, for power is made perfect in weakness.* —*2 Corinthians 12:9*

Yesterday afternoon I fixed the bottom porch step of my cabin. I worked carefully to make sure the step was perfectly straight.

Satisfied, I stepped back to admire my work and began to laugh! I was so intent on making sure the new step was straight that I didn't take into account that the other steps were crooked. The one straight step looked cock-eyed and out of place.

I continued to chuckle as I recalled the theme of my writing the day before—the interplay between small details and the big picture. Here was a perfect example of getting so caught up in one small piece of the picture that, when taken in context, it looked ridiculous. The other steps looked fine. It was my straight step that appeared out of place. I found myself explaining to a friend who stopped by that my step was actually the straight one lest she think poorly of my carpentry skills! I can just picture God gently laughing. I tend to take life seriously and would like to think I won't make the same mistake twice. When I inevitably repeat my mistakes, I'm harsh with myself. But this time I could laugh and enjoy the inconsistency of the fact that the day after writing theoretically about keeping details in global context, I build a simple step that doesn't fit!

Learning to laugh at myself is a sign of surrender— not a surrender to my mistakes but a giving up of my futile efforts to conquer them once and for all. I don't throw my hands up in despair and quit trying. Rather, I surrender to the God of love my mistakes, my efforts, my desire to do things right.

I'm amazed at God's words to Paul: "My grace is sufficient for you, for power is made perfect in weakness." It isn't that God simply makes do with my weakness. The verse says that God's power is made perfect in weakness.

I'll never forget the conversation in which a friend pointed out that God's power in its purest form would overwhelm us. Our weakness makes God's power softer and more malleable. What a concept! God chooses over and over again to need us. God chooses to come to us in human form, in weakness, and in vulnerability.

I find that I want to offer my strengths and gifts for God to use. But somehow I feel as if I need to get rid of my weaknesses. I need to change them into strengths before God can use them. The challenge is to surrender even my weaknesses to God, trusting that God laughs gently at my foibles and tries to teach me to do the same. Surrender, then, becomes not a sign of giving up but of giving over—giving over everything to the God whose power is made perfect in weakness.

Experiencing God's sense of humor helps me learn not to take myself and my weaknesses too seriously. How do you experience God's sense of humor? What do you think of the idea that God not only "makes do" with our weaknesses but chooses to need even our shortcomings?

# Freedom from Choices

*The secret of the spiritual life is the willingness to miss almost everything. —Unknown*

A NICARAGUAN FARMER visited the U.S. on an exchange program. When friends tried to convince him to stay in North America, he replied, "Why would I trade the freedom of my poverty for the slavery of your affluence?" I struggle to understand his words. Am I enslaved by affluence?

I've lived in Latin America since 1981. Returning to the U.S. every two years, I learned to prepare myself for feeling overwhelmed by the seemingly endless choices in grocery stores and restaurants.

Soon after returning to the U.S. for an extended sabbatical, I walked into a restaurant and experienced a breakthrough. I looked at the extensive food bar laden with foods of all kinds and realized I didn't have to make each choice a burdensome decision. I would simply move through the line, choose sizable portions of two or three items, and not worry about whether or not I made the best choices or missed something I should have tried. Even as I write, I smile. It sounds so simple and straightforward. Why was it such a freeing experience?

As a North American, I think I've learned to equate freedom with options. A store close to my home proudly advertises stocking 135 different cereals and 184 kinds of salad dressing. But too many options paralyze me! How can I "check out all the options" when there are so many from which to choose?

A visual image of a long hallway with many doors comes to mind. When most of the doors are open, I can't move down the hallway without checking out what is in each room. My energy is dissipated as I spend time exploring the many rooms. I'm unable to walk down the hall freely. But when most of the doors are closed, my energy has direction and focus.

In the process of adjusting to living in the U.S. again, I dedicated tremendous energy to daily decisions, such as buying clothes, choosing between brands of food, deciding which book to buy or borrow, which magazines to read.

Most families face major decisions as well. Time and energy are poured into choosing what car to drive, what house to live in, which appliances are needed. Some dedicate energy to those decisions because they are concerned to maintain an image acceptable to society. Others pour equal amounts of energy or more into the same decisions because they are concerned with living simply and responsibly. Then there are the career options among which we must select, not just as youth but over and over during our lifetime.

Several years ago, when I turned thirty-five, I realized abruptly that before long I would no longer have the option of bearing children. I thought back on the decisions I had made with my life and saw none I regretted. In my twenties I somehow thought I would be able to do everything—work long-term with MCC, marry, raise a family, dedicate myself to others, live a "normal" life. Now I'm realizing choices have consequences. Because I've chosen to dedicate myself to the poor, some options are no longer available. Ironically, I feel more and more free as I embrace the path that is mine to walk without being sidetracked by exploring every door I encounter. The prevalent attitude encouraging me to "keep my options open" is possible only at the expense of long-term commitment and direction for my life.

It's a natural human tendency to want it all, to resist accepting the consequences of making choices. A friend in Arizona said somewhat cynically that many people from the east move to Arizona because of the dry climate. But they also like green grass and flowers, so they water their lawns. So many people in Phoenix now water their lawns that the humidity level is rising. In trying to grab it all, we destroy the little given to us as gift.

Society would have me believe that there is a perfect option out there for me just waiting to be discovered. When life is hard and we can't find the perfect option we feel cheated and victimized. But freedom doesn't consist of spending life exploring the options available to me.

Jesus promised, "You will know the truth, and the truth will make you free." A friend wisely pointed out that Jesus doesn't promise to teach us true dogma but to make us true. I experience freedom as the Spirit makes me true—true to my call as a child of God to follow Jesus.

Following Jesus means accepting that the way is narrow. Walking faithfully day by day doesn't offer the lure of endless options. But the boundaries provided by committing myself to the narrow way don't enslave me. Rather, they provide the framework I need so my energy can flow with purpose and direction.

Being willing to "miss almost everything" is the secret to the spiritual life, because it enables me to live my own unique calling fully and deeply. How are you affected by options? How do you see the relationship between options and long-term commitments?

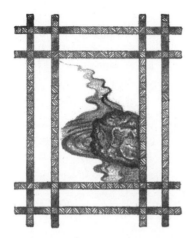

# Yardsticks and Measuring Cups

*Give, and it will be given to you. A good measure, pressed down, shaken together, running over, will be put into your lap; for the measure you give will be the measure you get back. —Luke 6:38*

I'M THINKING about the futility of trying to measure love and grace. In my concern with being effective and seeing the fruits of my work, I often try to measure the immeasurable.

Friends of mine have two biological children and one adopted child. When their biological children were infants, the couple lovingly lined an old trunk with blankets to use as a bassinet. But they bought a crib for their adopted child. Why? Because social workers need criteria for measuring love and using a trunk for a baby to sleep in doesn't meet standards!

Grace is as impossible to measure as love. I took a seminary course last year and wrote a paper on grace in

Anabaptism. It came as an exciting discovery to learn that the Anabaptists' understanding of discipleship was linked to their understanding of grace. I was excited because I grew up hearing a great deal about discipleship and very little concerning grace.

The Anabaptists believed that God's grace enabled them to grow more and more in the image of God. God's grace didn't simply take away punishment for their sin but changed their lives. And their changed lives found expression through discipleship—putting their faith into action. But our Anabaptist forebears and many Christians today find ourselves hung up with legalistic yardsticks, trying to measure how a life must change to prove we have genuinely experienced God's renewing grace.

I find myself drawn to Luke's assurance that "the measure you give will be the measure you get back" (Luke 6:38). As I think of examples of love and grace in my life, I'm sure the measure God uses is different from my own.

During my early years in El Salvador, I tried to express my love for the people by being effective and productive. I saw the health problems and worked hard to make an impact. But I was frustrated because I couldn't make a significant difference.

At one point I was caught in a battle. The bullets flew so close that the gravel spurted at my feet, and I saw two soldiers injured before my eyes. My frustration as I dealt with that experience wasn't that I could have been killed but that I was forced to recognize my powerlessness. I could work as hard as humanly possible, I could even give my life—yet little would change for the people I loved.

In the years that followed I saw that my inability to accept my powerlessness prevented me from accepting the love the people had for me. I couldn't accept myself, so I couldn't believe my friends loved and accepted me. As I surrendered my need to make a measurable difference, I began to experience God's immeasurable love and grace through the people I wanted so desperately to help.

Coming to terms with my powerlessness and letting go of measuring effectiveness according to my yardsticks are ongoing challenges in my life. I wonder what situations have brought you face-to-face with powerlessness. How do you respond to people and situations that remind you that you aren't in control?

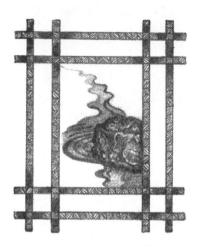

# A Melted Mask

*Let the same mind be in you that was in Christ Jesus,
who, though he was in the form of God, did not regard
equality with God as something to be exploited, but
emptied himself, taking the form of a slave, being born
in human likeness.* —Philippians 2:5-7

JESUS SURRENDERED the power available to him and chose
to come to us through vulnerability. I can't intellectually
understand God's power through vulnerability but I'm get-
ting better at recognizing examples of it. I'm thinking this
morning about an experience on a subway in Chicago.

It was only the second time I had been on the sub-
way, so I wasn't sure where I was going. I was glad for
the map in my hand. I had been in the city long enough
to observe the mask of indifference people paste on
their faces in city crowds.

When I sat down on the subway I noticed a woman
facing me whose mask was particularly impenetrable.
She didn't blink an eye when a woman squeezed past her

to sit on the seat next to her. Then the train started and I forgot the woman as I followed my map. At one point, however, I glanced up and saw she was watching me. Our eyes met, melting the mask of indifference frozen on her face. I smiled at her; she returned a sheepish grin. The obvious fact that I didn't know where I was going lowered her defenses, and we made a human connection. My heart danced with delight!

I remember a discussion with several college students in a city with a high crime rate. One young woman had recently been mugged. At the insistence of her friends, she began carrying a can of mace. "I couldn't walk down the street without looking at each person and wondering if I should pull the mace out of my purse," she said emphatically. She quit carrying it after a few days. The possibility of defending herself made her fearful and suspicious of the people around her. She didn't want to live her life in fear.

Choosing vulnerability doesn't mean being gullible and naive. It means standing firmly against the rules of the power struggle as defined by society and choosing to surrender to God's love. In Henri Nouwen's words, "A theology of weakness challenges us to look at weakness not as a worldly weakness that allows us to be manipulated by the powerful in society and church, but as a total and unconditional dependence on God."[5]

My natural reaction when I feel vulnerable is to put up defenses. Yet God consistently challenges me to let the defenses drop. I wonder what comes to mind when you think about being vulnerable. How have you experienced God's power through vulnerability?

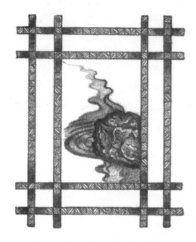

# Sidetracked Yearning

*As a deer longs for flowing streams, so my soul longs for you, O God. —Psalm 42:1*

FROM A DISTANCE I could see the top of what looked like abandoned train cars. Curious, I walked along the tracks until I could see them up close. The gutted cars had been pulled on to a parallel track. Broken glass and rusty metal littered my path.

Before being pulled toward the old cars I had been thinking about the yearning of my heart for God. As I poked through the train, I found my thoughts returning to the subject of longing for God. God plants in our hearts a longing only God can fulfill. But that longing for God is often sidetracked. A vague sense of dissatisfaction hints that there is more to life than what I'm experiencing. Society tells me that the "something more" can be found in prestige, possessions, acceptance, power, money. The list goes on.

I look again at the sidetracked train cars, empty and

abandoned. "Society's promises for fulfillment will end up like these cars," I think to myself. How God's heart must break watching us follow our inner yearnings down the wrong track.

Pilgram Marpeck, an early Anabaptist leader, called the innate longing for God "original grace." Original grace enables us to recognize the difference between good and evil and choose to turn toward Christ. I find the term original grace refreshing. My human nature may be fallen but God has provided a way out. What's more, according to Marpeck, creation itself is my teacher. "For everything that leads to godliness is good, and not evil, for all visible creatures are placed in the world as apostles and teachers."[6] Am I listening?

On two occasions I went to a mall to sit and pray. Malls are important places in North American society, and I wanted to be attentive to God's presence there. I sat quietly, watching, listening. I felt sad. As North Americans we value freedom and independence. Yet the longer I sat there the more I sensed the lack of freedom.

Who determines styles and colors? Who decides the length of skirts and the kinds of clothes available for me to buy? Yet styles are so important I even read of a teenager committing murder over a pair of "in" tennis shoes.

It had never occurred to me to wonder who decides that everything in my kitchen and bathroom has to be country blue one year and mauve the next. I realize, now, that I was passively surrendering to vague, unnamed forces—modern idols goading me to follow by promising that styles and possessions will meet my need for love and acceptance.

I suppose it's easy for me self-righteously to criticize malls and clothing styles. But what are my idols? I'm on the wrong track when I think the longing of my heart will be fulfilled through meeting the expectations of other people. I run into a dead end when I make a life of service my goal instead of first loving God with my heart and soul and mind. I could easily slide into dedicating myself to worthy causes and feeling as if I have to pick up the burden when others don't do their share.

But the nameless idols don't have to have the last word! Surrendering to the deepest longing of my heart disarms the idols and leads me toward God because God placed the longing within me. When I end up at another dead end, I know that I can try again, that God will honor my genuine efforts to be faithful. I can rest assured that God wants so much for me to turn toward my Creator that all of creation is my teacher.

I found it helpful to go to a mall to pray. You might want to try praying at a mall or bank. How do you experience God's presence there? What dead ends have you experienced as you follow the yearning of your heart?

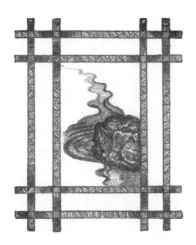

# Untangling

*The surprise of grace waits at the core of what I run from inside myself.* —Peter Campbell

I FEEL VULNERABLE today. Intellectual insights are easy to write and discuss. They are clear and neatly packaged. But for those seeds to take root in my heart I have to surrender to the truth and allow it to change me.

When Mary and I lived together in El Salvador, we made a commitment that has proven more significant than we realized at the time. We agreed to be mirrors, reflecting back what we see in each other. We share deeply and intimately; sometimes I don't like what I see. I can't hide when I see myself reflected through Mary's eyes. And when I find myself embarrassed by the reality present within me, I literally hang my head, averting my eyes from her compassionate gaze. That's when I know that when I reject myself I also reject God's love.

This week Mary has reflected back to me through tapes and letters the way my thoughts and feelings become tangled. I'm dealing with feeling anxious about a particular situation and find my mind spinning in circles. I arrive at a dead end and start over again. When will I learn?

Robert Johnson, in his book *Owning Your Own Shadow*, proposes that the cultural process involves sorting through our God-given characteristics defining some as acceptable to society and rejecting others. But the rejected characteristics don't disappear. Rather, they collect in the dark corners of our personality which Johnson calls the shadow. "It is . . . astonishing to find that some very good characteristics turn up in the shadow. . . . Some of the pure gold of our personality is relegated to the shadow because it can find no place in that great leveling process that is culture."[7] Is there gold somewhere in my jumbled thoughts?

Friends tell me they are grateful for the way I articulate thoughts and feelings they have trouble expressing. I don't need to feel ashamed that my muddled thoughts get snarled. I don't need to apologize for the energy it takes for me to make sense of them. The untangling process is what gives birth to clarity. It's the hidden nugget of gold, the surprise of grace, in a characteristic I find frustrating.

When I feel ashamed or embarrassed about myself, I need to look to see what I'm rejecting. Perhaps my gifts lie wrapped in the very characteristic I'm futilely trying to keep hidden in a dark corner. I take a deep breath and humbly recognize that my mind will spin in circles until the day I die, but sometimes the spinning will give birth to a simple, life-giving truth. And for that I'm grateful.

I wonder if you share my tendency to reject God's love when you reject yourself. What do you run from inside yourself? Is there a nugget of gold hidden there?

# The Wind and Sun

*Unless a grain of wheat falls into the earth and dies, it remains just a single grain; but if it dies, it bears much fruit.* —*John 12:24*

My FATHER lovingly taught me about letting go through his life and death. I was in the U.S. on home leave when the message came that my father had just been hospitalized because of a brain tumor. I returned to Ohio immediately and arrived minutes before Dad was wheeled off to surgery. He repeated the exact words my mother and he spoke when I was preparing to leave for Bolivia soon after learning that the cancer my mother had been fighting was beginning to spread. "Your mother and I dedicated you to God when you were a baby and we meant it," he told me. "You must be faithful to your call."

He said he didn't want or expect me to stay in the U.S. to care for him. He asked only that I allow him to cry when I left without fearing that his tears meant he was unable to let me go. They were the last clear words he ever spoke. The surgery left him an invalid, and he died eight months later. I'm left with an inspiring legacy of life-giving, enabling love.

Years later I'm still learning what it means to let go. I visited friends in October. It was three-year-old Alma's birthday and her aunt gave her a new book. The wind and sun see a man with his overcoat on to protect him from the cold. The wind boasts, "I'm so powerful I can force him to take off his coat!" The sun just smiles. The wind blows with great might but the man buttons his coat higher. The wind tries again unleashing powerful gusts but the man turns up his collar.

Now it's the sun's turn. The sun smiles gently on the man. He looks up gratefully and loosens the top button. The sun continues to bathe him until he becomes confident that he no longer needs his coat and takes it off.

Some of the most profound concepts are simple. Willpower and determination are strong like the wind but can't force me to let go of my defenses. But God, like the sun, warms me with love until I realize I don't need my hard outer shell. When I'm confident of God's love, I choose to let go and willingly trade my own protective coat for the security of God's love. God's love softens me just like the warm, damp earth softens the seed so the sprout can break through.

Surrendering to enabling love means letting go of my determination to do it right! Love invites me to relax. I will never achieve "surrender" but can walk the path.

Who are your role-models for love that lets go and enables? How do you experience the strength of the wind in your life? The gentle warmth of the sun?

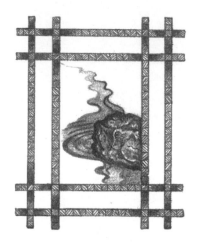

# Loving
# Myself
# and My
# Neighbor

*You shall love the Lord your God with all your heart,*
*and with all your soul, and with all your strength,*
*and with all your mind; and your neighbor as yourself.*
—*Luke 10:27*

I PARTICIPATED in a workshop for people who work with
those who are severely mentally and physically dis-
abled. I was particularly touched by the wisdom of one
young woman. She shared that at first it was difficult to
work with people with severe handicaps. She wondered
about the quality of their life and questioned the worth
of the life they lived. But then she began to recognize
that they were also created in God's image. She looked
for each one's special gift—a smile, laughter, wit.

Seeing God in the people she worked with changed
her perception of them. But the change went deeper
than her attitude toward others. As she recognized
God's image in others, she came to see God's image in
herself. Now when many of her peers are concerned

with how they look, she is able to relax in the confidence that she is created in the image of God.

The young woman's sharing provides a clear example of the dynamic process of loving ourselves and loving others. A friend who works with volunteers in a Christian organization mentioned that more and more people come with the attitude that they need to love themselves before they can love other people. The issue is a difficult one; it's true my ability to love myself affects my capacity to love others.

The question becomes "How do I learn to love myself?" The young woman working with severely disabled people came to a greater sense of self-love and acceptance as she loved and accepted others.

I like issues to be neat and orderly. I want the loose ends tied together before I start something new. But I have to smile when I think of putting self-love and acceptance on a list of tasks to accomplish! When will I ever be able to check that one off my list? Do I wait to love and serve others until my own issues are resolved?

It's important for me to surrender my desire to "achieve" inner growth as if it were a task to be completed. Instead, I need to look at my inner journey as a continuous process with its own cycles and rhythms. There will be times I need to withdraw and focus my energy on my own inner healing. But I must also recognize that my journey is connected with other people. As I learn to know and love the outcasts of society, I learn to know and love parts of myself I've relegated to the margins.

How have you experienced the relationship between loving yourself and loving others?

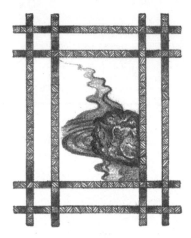

# Innocence and Wisdom

*See, I am sending you out like sheep into the midst of wolves; so be wise as serpents and innocent as doves.*
*—Matthew 10:16*

CHILDREN TEACH ME a great deal about the influences of society. Two examples come to mind.

I was delighted to spend several days with Maureen, my first MCC co-worker in El Salvador. She is now married and has two young children. My last evening with Maureen and her family, we managed to track down a slide projector so I could show them my slides from El Salvador. The slide presentation includes pictures of the war and massacres; about halfway through, I became acutely aware of the impact watching it might have on three-year-old Rachel.

Sure enough, at the end of the slides Rachel ran to her mother's lap. "Are the Indians going to kill me, too?" she asked fearfully. Afterwards Maureen and I talked about her fear. Rachel doesn't watch TV at home or at her babysitter's. Why would she be afraid of Indians? Where did she pick up the negative stereotype? Maureen could only guess that Rachel must have learned from neighborhood children that Indians are "bad guys."

Four-year-old Nathan also reflected a negative stereotype. He was riding in the car with his mother when he turned and asked, "Mommy, why are white people better than black?"

His mother was dumbfounded but tried to remain calm in her response. "How do you know white people are better than black?" she asked.

"Oh, I just know," he responded.

Nathan's family has no TV and his parents, like Rachel's, are exceptionally conscientious about teaching their children that God's love includes people from all cultures. The strength of society's influence is revealed by the fact that at age three and four they already reflect values that are opposite those of their parents. Some may argue that racism is no longer an issue but young children pierce the myth and reveal the fact that negative stereotypes still prevail.

When Jesus sent forth his disciples, he counseled them to be "wise as serpents and innocent as doves." I feel challenged by the way Jesus brings together wisdom and innocence. Nathan and Rachel innocently reveal society's stereotypes but don't yet have the wisdom to know that what society teaches is wrong. I need innocent vulnerability to perceive the reality present underneath smooth words and rational arguments. But I also need wisdom to help me sift through the lies.

Those with access to technology now have unlimited

information available at their fingertips. We are in the age of the "Information Super Highway." I find it important to remind myself, however, that knowledge isn't wisdom. Knowledge wields power and increases the gap between the "haves" and "have-nots." But the door to wisdom is open to anyone willing to walk the path of innocent vulnerability.

What have the children in your life taught you about the influences of our society? How do you experience the relationship between wisdom and innocence?

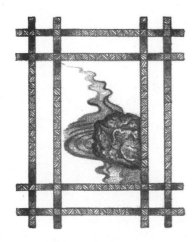

# Pursue Love

*And now faith, hope, and love abide, these three;*
*and the greatest of these is love. Pursue love. . . .*
*—1 Corinthians 13:13—14:1*

SEVERAL DAYS AGO I visited an older woman in a retirement home. At one point her face beamed with pleasure. "I'm so grateful," she said, "for the opportunity I have now to look back on my life and celebrate the love I've experienced."

She shared an example of love. Years before her sister was dying of tuberculosis. My friend's work requirements were strict but she remembered gratefully that her supervisors gave her two days off to spend with her dying sister.

I was amazed. She could have been bitter that her sister died so young. She could have resented the regulations that made even two days off an exception. But she saw love in the opportunity to spend even a short time with her sister.

Paul writes that love is greater than hope and faith. Hope energizes us as we try to embody God's love, and faith provides courage based on trust and vision as we seek to follow God. But nowhere does the Bible say that "God is hope" or "God is faith." The Bible does tell us, however, that "God is love" (1 John 8:15) and Paul explained to the people of Athens that in God "we live and move and have our being" (Acts 17:28). Gerald May sums it up well: "We are created by love, to live in love, for the sake of love."[8]

How can I become more aware of the love that created me, surrounds me, and longs to motivate me? Several obstacles come to mind. Pride keeps me from receiving love by trying to convince me I'm in control and capable of running my life.

Guilt is another obstacle. Guilt motivates me to act in ways that may appear loving while in reality I'm motivated by the desire to ease my discomfort. As I think about guilt in my life, I realize that much of it stems from looking for love and acceptance in a world that will never be my home.

Surrendering to love leads me to my real home—to the reason and purpose of my existence. Surrendering to love puts me in touch with God who is love. I'm then free energetically to dedicate all I have and all I am to God. I only feel guilty when I try to justify holding back.

Paul tells us to "pursue love." How do I do it? By yielding to God in whom I live, move, and have my being.

How can you become more aware of the love that created you, surrounds you, and longs to motivate you? How are you affected by pride and guilt?

# A Rooted Identity

Self-identity is a crucial
issue. I learn to love
and accept myself as I
experience the dignity
of being created in
the image of God.
But God didn't create
me to be autonomous
and self-sufficient.
I am connected to all
of God's creation
and will only flourish
as I dedicate myself
and my gifts to
the common good.

# Connected
# Threads

*When we tug at a single thing in nature, we find it at-
tached to the rest of the world.* — *Unknown*

I HAD RECENTLY returned to North America when I read
an anonymous letter in a Mennonite publication. The
writer stated four issues were crucial in his life and asked
why he had never heard them addressed in the church.
The first issue was his struggle with low self-esteem.

I have no solutions for him but his question helped
direct my thoughts and observations during the year that
followed. It quickly became apparent that the anony-
mous writer wasn't alone in his struggle with low self-
esteem. Why is it so difficult for him, for me, for the
many of us who deal with identity issues to confidently
recognize that we reflect God's image?

I'm thinking, this morning, about three ways the influ-
ences of American society make it difficult for me to rec-
ognize my God-given identity. Teka has lived and worked
for years in a Catholic Worker community in St. Louis. In

reflecting on the influences of American society she commented, "Society teaches that to be human is to have goods." In other words, "We are what we own." An identity based on what we own is as destructive for those who can afford the goods as for the ones who can't.

I was struck by a credit card advertisement that articulated a critical question. "What's in it for me?" the headline demanded in bold letters. Self-centered attitudes prevent me from recognizing that fulfillment depends on my willingness to use my gifts for their intended purpose. God gives us each gifts to use, not for individualistic gain but for the common good.

The United States Constitution assures us the right of "life, liberty, and the pursuit of happiness." Ironically, it's the very pursuit of happiness that guarantees it will elude my grasp. When I make happiness my goal, I avoid the characteristics the gospel declares bring genuine life and blessing—willingness to surrender, suffer, experience persecution, walk the narrow path. Happiness is the fruit of a faithful life, not a goal to be pursued. No wonder so many of us struggle with low self-esteem!

A healthy self-identity depends on recognizing that I'm not autonomous or self-sufficient. The directory of a Catholic community of religious women has a picture of a plant on the front with the words, "When we tug at a single thing in nature we find it attached to the rest of the world." God created the universe as an interconnected whole. Tugging at the thread of self-identity, I find it attached to the rest of the world and to God.

My identity is based on a personal relationship with

God. The influences of society too often co-opt an *individual* relationship, making it an *individualistic* one. Through deep personal relationship with God I learn how I uniquely reflect God's image and become aware of the gifts that God has given me.

A positive self-identity, then, isn't based on the assumption that to be human is to have goods, but on the truth that to be human is to reflect God's image. The critical question isn't "What's in it for me?" but "What gifts do I have to offer the common good?" My goal isn't to pursue happiness but to surrender my life to God.

Experiencing our connectedness is a challenge. Some tend to avoid the inner work of personal growth, judging it an escape from the crucial issues of peace and justice. Others lose the broad connectedness to those issues by focusing primarily on the narrow pursuit of individual growth. While our giftedness is apt to be stronger in one area than the other, we must all recognize that justice issues and our inner personal journey are inseparable.

I wonder how you experience the connection between working for justice and coming to a deeper understanding of yourself as a child of God. How do you think society's values influence self-identity?

# Roots

*For there is hope for a tree, if it is cut down, that it will
sprout again. —Job 14:7*

I WAS FASCINATED by the variety of plants in the desert.
How do they survive? I learned that the scrubby mes-
quite tree sends its roots straight down looking for a wa-
ter source before it begins to grow above ground. When
workers were drilling a well they found a mesquite tree
with roots 175 feet deep! The saguaro cactus guarantees
its survival using a different approach. The roots don't
grow down but out. The root system is superficial, ex-
tending outward to take advantage of the occasional
ground water which the cactus stores.

The mesquite tree and saguaro cactus teach me that
survival depends on my root system. Indigenous Guate-
malans have a saying, "They yanked off our fruit. They cut
our branches. They burned our trunk. But they couldn't
destroy our roots." When Ann was celebrating her twen-
ty-fifth anniversary as a nun, I embroidered a banner for

her with those words. Two years later, her mother gave
it back to me after Ann died of cancer.

Job was despondent as he described mortals like flow-
ers that wither and shadows that pass. But he saw trees
differently. "For there is hope for a tree, if it is cut down,
that it will sprout again, and its shoots will not cease.
Though its root grows old in the earth, and its stump
dies in the ground, yet at the scent of water it will bud
and put forth branches like a young plant" (Job 14:7-9).

A plant with roots intact can't be destroyed. It's a
struggle for me to let go of my preoccupation with bear-
ing fruit, being productive, seeing results. But nature
teaches me to nurture the slow, quiet growth of Christ
taking root within me. The growth and fruit naturally
follow the cycles of nature when my roots are healthy.
I rejoice when I see new sprouts and ripening fruit in
my life, but they are beyond my control.

Like the mesquite tree, my roots need to grow straight
down to receive nourishment from God, the Source of
life and growth. And like the saguaro cactus, my roots
need to extend outward along the surface of the ground
drawing nourishment by reaching out to the people
around me.

I wonder how you would describe your root system.
How are you nourished by your relationship with God?
By relationships with others?

# Looking
# in the
# Mirror

*For it was you who formed my inward parts; you knit me together in my mother's womb.* —*Psalm 139:13*

MARY AND I visited a support group for women who have been in jail. I left the meeting thrilled and inspired. There was a tangible sense of hope as the women challenged, taught, and cared for each other.

A woman who I will call Sandra shared her story. She was pregnant by the time she was sixteen, married for ten years to a man who beat her, addicted to drugs, and eventually imprisoned for covering up a drug traffic ring. While in prison, Sandra had opportunity to participate in a drug rehabilitation program. A friend in the program gave her a mirror. "At first I couldn't look in that mirror," Sandra shared. "Finally I was able to look in the mirror and know that God made me. I learned who I really am."

Her words moved me when I listened to her share and again as I write. I just got up and looked in a mirror. You might want to try it as well. As I gazed in the mirror, I thought about the fact that I have been created in the image of God. "For it was you who formed my inward parts; you knit me together in my mother's womb" (Ps. 139:13).

Tears come to my eyes. I have been created in God's image, knit together by God, my Creator. Yet how often I try to conform to the image and expectations of others or strain to make myself into an image I create for myself.

"What does it mean to know yourself as created in the image of God?" a friend asked. I ponder the question. What do I know about God? God is love. God is my Creator, the Author of life. God, the Omnipotent, chose to surrender power, chose to need us, chose to nurture intimacy with us by coming to us in human form. Jesus' death and resurrection indicate the way God infuses life into pain and death.

Knowing myself to be created in God's image, then, means being rooted in love. It means recognizing that God gifts each one of us with life-giving creativity. Being created in God's image means getting in touch with my vulnerability and knowing myself as an individual in relationship with all of creation. It means following the path of pain and death to experience resurrected life.

I wonder how you would answer the question "What does it mean to know yourself as created in the image of God?" What impact would it make on your life if you could look in a mirror and say like Sandra, "I know God made me"?

# Trusting Myself

*A religious experience is not something abnormal. . . .*
*It is simply an experience with a religious interpreta-*
*tion. —Albert Nolan*

A FRIEND WAS CONCERNED that her four-year-old son have
opportunity to see women in professional roles, so she
chose a woman dentist and pediatrician. One day when
Jamie was putting a bandage strip on his teddy bear,
Kori asked if he wanted to be a doctor when he grew
up. "Oh, Mom," he replied condescendingly. "Only girls
can be doctors."

I love the story and enjoy telling it. But it's more than
a funny story about a mother's effort that backfired. I'm
challenged by the way Jamie trusted his experience and
drew on it to reach his own conclusions.

I have trouble trusting my own experience. When I
write I have to be careful of my tendency to use too
many quotes from other people. It's as if my ideas aren't
reliable unless corroborated by someone else.

When I began my sabbatical with six months of solitude and reflection in rural Kentucky, I thought I would finally have time to read all the books on my long list of "someday" books. But interestingly enough, I didn't do much reading during those months. I didn't need more input. I needed to digest my experiences, integrate them into my life, and listen to the Spirit speaking to me through them. I processed through journaling, writing, and working with my hands.

Any experience can be an opportunity to learn and grow when I take the time to listen to it, interpret it in the light of Scripture, and incorporate it into my life. I need to remind myself of that over and over because my tendency is to give priority to ideas rather than experience. It's part of my struggle with trusting my intellect at the expense of my heart and gut.

When Jamie concluded that only girls could be doctors, Kori reminded him that both his grandfather and his uncle were physicians. I hope he recognized that his initial conclusion was too narrow but he could continue to trust his experience in reaching a different outcome.

I also hope I can learn to trust my everyday experiences, not narrowly defining my conclusions as the only ones, but trusting what is true for me even as I open myself to what is true for others.

I wonder if you share my tendency to trust the experiences and thoughts of other people more than your own. How do you process everyday events so they become opportunities to listen to the Spirit?

# Raising Food Is Hard Work!

*You visit the earth and water it. . . .You water its furrows abundantly, settling its ridges, softening it with showers, and blessing its growth.* —Psalm 65:9-10

A FRIEND WAS VISITING El Salvador when Mary and I were working up the worthless clay ground behind our house, hoping to raise a garden. After watching us slashing at the hard soil with a pick and a hoe, she read us a verse from Psalm 65 in which God promises to break up the clods and saturate the earth with showers. "Breaking up the clods" became our theme as we slaved over a garden that pigs, ants, and drought threatened to destroy.

Producing something, anything, became a matter of principle. When water was scarce, we realized the importance of hoeing around each plant so the precious drops would nourish the roots and not run off into the weeds. When army ants stripped four cabbages of leaves, Mary got up in the middle of the night to follow the pillagers to their home where she sprinkled poison.

When pigs got in we chased them out, patching the holes in our makeshift bamboo fence with dogged determination. We hauled manure from the pasture to fertilize the ground and worked sawdust in to break up clods. We gratefully celebrated our first real produce: big, red juicy tomatoes.

Raising food is hard work! If Mary and I had to depend on what we could raise we would starve. My spiritual nourishment also takes time and effort. I can't go grocery shopping, picking off the shelves ready-made mixes to meet every spiritual need.

During my early years in El Salvador, I worked with severely malnourished children. Malnutrition has several causes. We often think of malnutrition due to lack of food or not eating the proper kinds of food. But malnutrition can also be caused by the body's inability to absorb available nutrients.

In the U.S. I'm surrounded with opportunities for spiritual nourishment but also by influences that make it hard for me to absorb the nutrients I need. Several examples come to mind. Society emphasizes ease, comfort, and convenience. But spiritual nourishment requires discipline, perseverance, and hard work. Society places priority on efficiency, results, and speed. But spiritual nourishment tends to be slow, emphasizing process more than end product. Society demands more and more options while spiritual nourishment requires that I walk the narrow path of my unique calling.

I appreciate the image the psalmist uses. God wants to water the ground of my heart settling and softening the hardened ridges. God doesn't use the force of torrential downpours because hard rain falling on parched ground runs off in flash floods. Rather, the ground of my heart is slowly saturated by God's soft, gentle showers. May my heart be open to absorb more and more of God's love and grace.

Think about your current spiritual nutritional status. What do you find nourishing? How do you think the values of society influence our expectations for spiritual **nourishment?**

# Candle Wax and Mosaic Tiles

*But even the hairs of your head are all counted. Do not be afraid; you are of more value than many sparrows.*
*—Luke 12:7*

CURIOUS ABOUT WHAT the encyclopedia says about the U.S., I looked up "United States." I learned interesting facts but was intrigued by the comments on personal choice and peer pressure. *Compton's Encyclopedia* mentions that individual choice and personal achievement are important to Americans but we place priority on choosing what is popular and acceptable to the majority. It's an interesting contrast between individualism on the one hand and following the crowd on the other.

The description of the American "melting pot" is fitting for a culture where peer pressure defines the boundaries of individual expression.

An example from El Salvador comes to mind. Mary and I helped start a small cottage industry in which women learned to work with leather and make candles.

The woman responsible for pouring candle wax into clay pots wanted to waste none so she would pour all the brightly colored leftover wax together, melt it down, and use it again. When we noticed the wax was dull and gray we explained that she needed to keep the leftover colors separate. We thought the problem solved. Months later, however, we realized she had started filling the pots with the old gray wax before adding a superficial layer of bright color on top to make it look pretty!

I can't help but wonder if the gray candle wax describes our U.S. melting pot. Are we becoming gray? Is the color of our individual identity shallow and superficial? A Canadian friend explained that Canada uses the image of a mosaic to describe themselves. The individual tiles of a mosaic create a picture without sacrificing individual distinctiveness.

Jesus assured his followers of their importance to God by telling them that "Even the hairs of your head are all counted" (Luke 12:7). It's clear that my relationship with God is deeply personal. God knows me as a unique individual. But I'm not the only 'one God knows as a unique individual! Perhaps in our tendency toward individualism we place ourselves at the center. We search for our identity within and try to prove our independence instead of celebrating our interdependence.

My God-given identity isn't a superficial layer of bright color. It's genuine and authentic through and through. In living out my true identity I don't fit in by trying to be like everyone else or by staying within parameters defined by the majority. I find myself by discovering the unique place where my tile fits in the mosaic made up of countless individual tiles.

How do you distinguish between an individual relationship with God and individualism valued by society?

# My Origin and Purpose

*This is what is meant by a prayerful life. It is not a life in which we say many prayers, but a life in which nothing, absolutely nothing, is done, said, or understood independently of [God] who is the origin and purpose of our existence.* —Henri Nouwen

I READ AN ARTICLE recently which explained the Greek word for truth. The literal translation for truth in Greek is "not forgetting" or "remembering." I find the connection challenging. Remembering helps keep me true.

In Numbers 15, God instructs Moses to tell the people to put fringes on their garments as symbols reminding them of God's commandments. Symbols hold great potential as life-giving reminders. What symbols are important to me? I have a small cedar cross I whittled out of a twig I found on the ground. I carry it in my pocket and find that rubbing it between my fingers helps me focus and concentrate when I pray. Seeing my little cross or feeling it in my pocket reminds me that God is the desire of my heart.

It isn't hard to think of examples of symbols and traditions that have lost their meaning. They eventually become rigid and are no longer life-giving reminders because symbols have no power in and of themselves. Their power lies in their capacity to remind us of God. When my little cedar cross no longer reminds me of my desire to pray then I will need to let go of it and find a new reminder.

God encourages us to remember and God also remembers. In Genesis 9:15 God says, "I will remember my covenant that is between me and you and every living creature . . . and the waters shall never again become a flood to destroy all flesh." In remembering the covenant, God makes a promise that influences the course of history. How can I make sure that the promises I make continue to influence my life?

I try to celebrate dates that mark important commitments in my life. One date I remember yearly is July 19. It's the day when a unique experience in a health promoter training course brought me to the point of formalizing my commitment to the poor. I articulated my commitment in the presence of the Salvadoran peasants attending the course. Remembering that date and other milestones in my life helps keep my commitments alive and relevant.

Henri Nouwen suggests that we are called to remind each other of the ways the human story and divine story are connected. Remembering the connection reminds me that my life isn't isolated but rooted in God. Nouwen writes, "This is what is meant by a prayerful life. It is not a life in which we say many prayers, but a life in which nothing, absolutely nothing, is done, said, or understood independently of [God] who is the origin and purpose of our existence."[9]

The symbols I choose, the commitments I make, the ways I remember are life-giving when they remind me that God is "the origin and purpose of my existence."

How do you remind yourself that God is the origin and purpose of your existence?

# Through God's Eyes

*Can a woman forget her nursing child, or show no
compassion for the child of her womb? Even these
may forget, yet I will not forget you.* —Isaiah 49:15

NOT BEING ACCUSTOMED to big cities, I felt a little inse-
cure the morning I set out alone to find my way to
downtown Chicago on public transportation. I got on the
train and easily found a seat on the almost empty car.

Then a young man boarded. I observed him out of
the corner of my eye. He was dressed in a black leath-
er jacket. His hair was slicked back. The evening before
I had spoken with two friendly teenagers who I learned
afterward were gang members. I was surprised. They
didn't fit my stereotypes. My active mind began spinning
out scenarios for the young man on the train. He didn't
quite fit my image of a gang member but then neither
did the two I met the evening before.

Then I remembered what I had just read in my morn-
ing quiet time, Isaiah 49:15. "Can a woman forget her

nursing child, or show no compassion for the child of her womb? Even these may forget, yet I will not forget you." The maternal image of God's love spoke to me. I felt challenged to look at the young man sitting in front of me with the eyes of a mother. What did his mother see when she looked at him? What difference might it make in my response to people if I practiced the discipline of trying to see them through their mothers' eyes?

The train pulled away. The stranger, whom I now felt kindly toward, pulled out a book. I glanced at the title. It was a Spanish version of *An Introduction to Biblical Hermeneutics*! My heart danced with delight at the unexpected surprise. I imagined God smiling at the gentle but clear lesson.

A friend with whom I shared the incident said, "I've had that sort of experience before, too—it makes me feel God is ready to help us break down barriers all the time, if we're just ready to see it."

How can I open myself to God's desire to break down the barriers? I seem to be more open when experiencing something new. I'm more alert, more observant, more aware of my dependence on God. Once I feel comfortable I quickly get in a rut and stop "seeing." Then I need consciously to remind myself to ask God to help me see the people around me.

Trains, subways, bus stations, and Laundromats are places where God helps me break through barriers. I wonder how you would respond to my question, "How can I open myself to God's desire to break down barriers?"

# Homeless but Not Nameless

*I have called you by name, you are mine.*
—Isaiah 43:1

THE CONTACT I've had with homeless people during the past few months has helped me recognize the significance of being called by name.

I met Daryll Scott last summer when I was visiting a friend in South Chicago. I walked out of Ingrid's apartment and noticed a man coming toward me. I clutched my purse and pasted on the blank mask of indifference I noticed on so many faces in the city. But the man was undeterred. He headed straight for me. Stereotypes of poor people in the inner city flashed through my mind; I wondered if I was about to be mugged.

Now he was calling me. "Excuse me, ma'am."

I stopped.

The man before me looked more despairing than threatening. He stared at his feet as he explained that he needed money. He spoke quickly, apparently afraid I wouldn't take the time to listen.

When I had a chance I broke in. "What's your name?" The man's head shot up in surprise. Looking me straight in the eye he held out his hand for me to shake.

"My name is Daryll Scott," he said smiling. "What's yours?"

"Susan," I replied with no trace of the fear that had gripped me a moment before.

The stereotypes vanished. I no longer saw him as a homeless beggar. We knew each others' names. A bond had been established. We visited with each other for five or ten minutes. I listened to his story and asked some questions. Then I gave him a little money, not out of fear or coercion but out of caring. We embraced and went our separate ways.

There was lightness in my step but heaviness in my heart as I walked away from Daryll. I celebrated the unexpected human connection with someone very different from myself as I thought about what he told me. I'm not naive. Many of the details of his story were likely false. But I believe he was truthful in saying he was homeless and hungry, that his feet hurt, that he wanted to break free from alcohol and hold a steady job. I suppose the tears of gratitude that filled his eyes could have been contrived, but I'm sure his spontaneous reaction when I asked his name was genuine.

I thought more about the heaviness. Such delight at simply being recognized as a human being can only come from someone who has experienced degradation and humiliation. Earlier I had visited a shelter where a letter from a homeless man was posted on the wall. He wrote that he appreciated the shelter because the staff knew his name. Those who have been dehumanized know the power of being called by name. The Bolivians I used to work with also understood the power of being named. The infant mortality rate was so high that many of the poor didn't name their babies until they were several months old and therefore more likely to live. By not naming a baby they feared would die, the parents hoped not to get too attached. With the name came acceptance of the child as a human being to be loved and nurtured.

Making a human connection with Daryll reminded me of the times when that essential element was missing. Sometimes I've hidden behind good development theory to escape the pain of looking another human being in the eye and saying no to their request. It's easier to say no when there isn't a relationship established.

I can also escape the vulnerability of a personal relationship through what appear to be acts of charity. My first thought when Daryll approached was to give him money quickly to get rid of him.

Sometimes I help others out of fear or guilt. I pray for the insight to discover how to make a human connection with people in need and the wisdom to know when a loving response is giving what they ask and when love means saying no.

Will I give money to the next person who asks? Maybe. Maybe not. I'm not even sure I should have given Daryll money. But I *am* sure that just as God lovingly calls me by name so must I call others by name as I recognize that we belong to the same family of God.

How does the fact that God calls you by name affect the way you feel about yourself? What can you do to encounter the human beings who live anonymously behind statistics and stereotypes?

# Structural Evil and Structural Grace

*We often talk of structural evil. Why don't we talk about structural grace? —Jon Sobrino*

LIVING THROUGH the civil war in El Salvador challenged me to think about structural evil. It was clear that evil structures are worse than the sum of their parts. I saw the human faces of soldiers who were mostly peasant farmers forced into the army against their will. Individually they were decent but collectively capable of massacres.

I was arrested by the government military and taken to the local barracks. There was a mural on the wall of a skull and crossbones with a slogan glorifying death. I shuddered as I sensed the presence of evil. The bench where I was sitting was close to the pay phone. It was mother's day in El Salvador, and I listened as soldier after soldier called his wife or mother expressing love and appreciation. Yes, these men were human beings. I knew, though, that at the shout of an order they could turn off their human side and become machines obeying orders to maim, kill, and torture.

Evil depends on human beings becoming machines. When I become mechanical, when I become numb, when I surrender my capacity to think and feel, when I give in to the "rush" of power even for a good cause, I too become capable of evil.

Because I've thought about structural evil I was struck by a comment made by Jon Sobrino, a Latin American theologian. "We often talk of structural evil," he said. "Why don't we talk about structural grace?" The concept had never occurred to me! But once I began thinking about it I easily came up with life-giving examples.

Friends and I faced a painful and delicate issue. The problem was overwhelming. Yet by the end of the afternoon we sensed God's grace had granted us wisdom. "Where two or three are gathered in my name, there I am in the midst of you," Jesus said. That is structural grace.

Other experiences of grace and community come to mind. I belong to the Support Circle, a scattered community of thirteen single Mennonite women spread out all over the world. We share a commitment to people who are marginalized and maintain our relationship with each other through letters and yearly retreats for those who can attend. The structure is minimal but God's life-giving grace flows through our common commitment.

When the problems of our world threaten to overwhelm me, I find it helpful to remind myself that grace is as real as evil. The undercurrent of grace flows through people, institutions, and cultures tapping into a potential for good that we can't touch as individuals.

How have you experienced structural grace?

# A Strand
# in the Web

*We did not weave the web of life; we are merely
a strand in it. Whatever we do to the "we," we do
to ourselves.* — *Chief Seattle*

IF I BELIEVE I'm a strand in the web of life, then I know
I'm affected by the other strands even when the effects
aren't immediately apparent. I'm thinking of an example
from the village where I lived in El Salvador. Mario is a
talented young man who is deaf and mute. For years I
knew him as a tailor and shoemaker. It wasn't until Mary
and I asked him to help teach several women to work
with leather that Mario had an opportunity to develop
his artistic talent.

I didn't sit around thinking about how much we were
missing because there was no artist in our village. But
my life has been enriched by the fact that Mario was fi-
nally given an opportunity to use his gift. The journal
cover he made for me is a reminder of the way we all
benefit when each person is able to flourish. We don't

consciously miss what we've never experienced but our lives are diminished nonetheless.

I'm drawn to the wisdom in Chief Seattle's words. "Whatever we do to the 'we,' we do to ourselves." Knowing myself within the "we," I recognize that there isn't competition between nurturing myself and caring for others. But it's a challenge to uncover the ways divisions have been imposed.

Some forms of theology encourage self-denial while forgetting that what is best for the common good is also best for me. Since I belong to the whole, I benefit from what I give. Taking up my cross is meant to be life-giving!

Society tends to emphasize caring for ourselves as if we were isolated individuals. Caring for myself then becomes selfish and self-centered. But if I recognize that we are all strands in the web, I know I can't genuinely care for myself at the expense of others. Caring for myself includes tending the web to which I belong.

The most common way I've heard of resolving the dilemma is to promote caring for ourselves first so we can help others. While I recognize and appreciate the truth that I can't give to others if I'm depleted, I find the advice doesn't take our fundamental unity into account. If I'm truly convinced I belong to the web of life and each strand has a unique gift, I will naturally nourish my gifts to be used for the common good. I know I have the most to offer when I'm rested, healthy, and energized.

My life was enriched when Mario had a chance to use his gifts. I mourn the loss of gifts that poverty and injustice never allow to develop. I also mourn the loss of gifts that low self-esteem prevents from being recognized or offered. And we all suffer when individualistic self-interest prevents some from committing their gifts to the common good. The whole body of Christ is diminished when individualism, injustice, or low self-esteem keep us from freely offering our gifts to each other.

How do you understand what it means to belong to the "we"? I wonder if you have gifts that haven't yet been developed or offered for the common good. What holds you back?

# Of Course They're Special!

*But you do see! Indeed you note trouble and grief,*
*that you may take it into your hands; the helpless*
*commit themselves to you; you have been the helper*
*of the orphan. —Psalm 10:14*

I STOPPED WRITING to go check my mail. To my surprise and delight, I had several letters from people in one of the Salvadoran villages where I worked.

My heart overflows with gratitude for the letters written painstakingly on scraps of notebook paper. I appreciate letters from friends no matter who they are or where they live. But these letters are special. I can picture my friends in the village of Los Calles consulting with each other. The person who writes the best will write the letter while the family gathers around adding comments and greetings. Two of the letters came in homemade envelopes fastened with masking tape. One letter was decorated with stars. Another included a poem. I'm deeply moved by letters from Salvadoran peasants because I know they are sincere. How can I explain the special love God has for people suffering on the margins of society? God's love is not exclusive. God loves the rich, poor, helpless, and powerful. But I believe God's heart goes out to those who are powerless just as a parent's heart fills with compassion for a helpless child. The psalmist notes that God is moved by trouble and grief. The helpless commit themselves to God and God is committed to them.

I'm thinking about several people in the village where I lived. Since their needs touched my heart and soul, I have no trouble believing God's compassionate heart reaches out to them in a special way.

Reyes is learning disabled and speech impaired. Since she has no family and no one to look out for her, Reyes' survival depends on the generosity of her neighbors. Choncito lived in a nearby village and died several weeks ago. He was also totally dependent on the kindness of others. Catalina is elderly and almost blind. She lives with her alcoholic son who beats her and takes the food the neighbors share with her.

When reminded of them I think, *Of course they hold a special place in God's heart! They have no one else.*

Every year 40 million people die from hunger and hunger-related diseases. That's equivalent to 300 jumbo jet crashes every day for a year.[10] Can you imagine the public outcry, the outrage if 300 jumbo jets crashed every day? But the people who die of hunger are different from those who die in airplanes. The people who die of hunger are poor. Their cries aren't heard. Their deaths aren't felt, at least not by society. But God feels each death and God's heart breaks with the pain of injustice. I wonder who comes to your heart as you think about people with special needs. Maybe it's someone who is terminally ill or severely disabled. What do they teach you about God's love?

# Authenticity

*Blessed are the pure in heart, for they will see God.*
*—Matthew 5:8*

I'M THINKING OF A WOMAN in the village where I lived in El Salvador. Reyes would be the kind of person many people would assume has nothing to contribute. She is elderly, hard of hearing, speech impaired, learning disabled. Yet when I think of Reyes, I think of a much needed characteristic in our world: authenticity. Reyes is real.

She stopped by our house one afternoon before we knew each other well. Since I was aware that she depended on the generosity of neighbors for food, I offered her some bread.

"You feel sorry for me," she said offended.

"We're friends," I replied.

A smile wreathed her face as she nodded her head affirmatively. "We're friends," she repeated accepting the bread.

On another occasion she had two bananas in her pocket when she stopped in for her almost daily visit. She handed me one. "Friends," she said again. "Yes," I nodded. I could tell by the way Reyes walked across the porch whether she was happy or angry. Reyes didn't need to read pop psychology books on the importance of expressing feelings or "being real." She was always genuine. Neighbors treated me with respect since I was an educated foreigner. But Reyes' authenticity and vulnerability accomplished what my power couldn't. She brought out what was real in other people. The way people treated Reyes broke through the facades and revealed their hearts.

Some who appeared responsible adults teased her mercilessly. About a month before Mary and I left our village for the U.S., we returned from a short trip to the city. Reyes arrived to greet us and burst into uncontrollable sobs. Little by little we learned why. Someone played a cruel joke on her by telling her we had left for good. But others who appeared gruff and indifferent treated her with kindness and compassion. Authenticity strips away the masks. No wonder it's a characteristic not highly valued by a world concerned with image, degrees, and success.

I think now about myself. What prevents me from being authentic? Trying to please others or meet their expectations certainly keeps me from being free. I also have a host of internal expectations that define who I "should" be. The "should" voice within me is critical and judgmental, complaining that who I am isn't good enough. I sacrifice authenticity when I give in to those harsh voices.

Sometimes there is an internal power struggle within me. I don't want to be vulnerable and powerless. It's too risky. I cruelly reject my vulnerability in the same way adults and children cruelly tease Reyes. Authentic compassion toward others can only flow from authentic compassion towards myself.

The pure in heart see God and reflect God through their transparent authenticity. I pray, O God, for the simplicity of a genuine and pure heart.

What keeps you from being authentic?

# Laundromats

*Let the oppressed see it and be glad; you who seek God,*
*let your hearts revive. For the Lord hears the needy,*
*and does not despise his own that are in bonds.*
—*Psalm 69:32-33*

DURING MY SABBATICAL in the U.S., I washed my clothes
at the Laundromat from time to time. It was a good ex-
perience. My family had a washer and dryer when I was
growing up and most of my friends do as well. It never
occurred to me before my sabbatical to think about the
many people who wash in Laundromats.

I have the option in North America of living my life
isolated from my neighbors. Before going to Latin Amer-
ica it was the only life I knew, but now I realize that I
miss the natural interaction that occurs when technology
doesn't offer the option of self-sufficiency. My favorite
time of day was at dusk, when the women would gather
at the public water faucet to fill the day's last water jug.
The soft light from the setting sun infused a quiet glow
into the trees and grass scorched by the mid-day heat.

Work was finished for the day and people visited freely. Washing my clothes by hand at the public wash sink provided a chance to visit with my neighbors and using public transportation kept me grounded in the reality of slow, overcrowded buses. The six-mile trip from my village to town took two hours walking, an hour-and-a-half in bus, or thirty minutes in car!

It was sometimes tempting to wish I had a vehicle of my own. Just think of the time I could save and the work I could accomplish! But the truth is, I didn't want my own car. Relationships were forged as I waited for buses with my neighbors, rode squashed together on the back of dusty trucks, and walked from place to place. Public transportation was inefficient in terms of accomplishing tasks but a very efficient way to relate to those who don't have private vehicles!

But yesterday I wasn't in the mood to enjoy washing at the Laundromat. I was in a hurry and the Laundromat wasn't efficient. I felt frustrated. Water flooded the floor because someone didn't close a washer door correctly, the dryer overheated, and a woman started smoking a cigarette when I was folding my freshly washed clothes!

Sometimes, though, I'm able to put efficiency in perspective and enter prayerfully into the lives of others who are waiting for their laundry. I feel compassion for mothers who seem harried and frustrated as they fight with mounds of dirty clothes stuffed into garbage bags. They lash out at their children who pay no attention. What is life like for those women who don't have the option of an efficient washer and dryer at home? Who does God see?

A question echoes in my mind. How will I use the many options available to me? It was hard to explain to people in El Salvador why I chose not to have a vehicle when it was assumed that all foreigners have their own cars. It doesn't make sense to wash in the Laundromat either if I have another option. Laundromats are expensive. But I make some choices because I need the perspective of people who don't have options.

Most people are on the margins of society because circumstances forced them there. When circumstances change, they "climb the ladder," acquiring as much wealth and prestige as possible. A poor Salvadoran village is a microcosm of global injustice. The same dynamics of power and wealth are visible on a micro level as the poor oppress the poorer.

I try to identify with society's outcasts, not because circumstances force me to the margins, but because God has called me there. Interestingly enough, as I relate to those rejected by society I get in touch with the parts of myself that I reject and relegate to the margins. I discover that God's special concern for the weakest and neediest includes my own pain and brokenness.

I find that if I'm not careful I surround myself with people who share my perspective on life. I need to make conscious choices to get in touch with perspectives different than mine.

I wonder how much variety there is among the people with whom you interact. What do you do to gain the perspective of people on the margins of society? How does interacting with those on the fringes put you in touch with your own issues of self-rejection?

# Connections

*Now there are varieties of gifts, but the same Spirit; and there are varieties of services, but the same Lord; and there are varieties of activities, but it is the same God who activates all of them in everyone. To each is given the manifestation of the Spirit for the common good.*
*—1 Corinthians 12:4-7*

I REMEMBER WALKING to a neighboring village with an MCC friend who was visiting Mary and me for several days. We were talking and laughing as we walked when suddenly our visitor burst out, "I think you two are long lost twins!" I enjoyed the comment then and now because it speaks to me of discovering our connectedness.

We often use the phrase "making connections" but I've come to appreciate thinking about "discovering connections" rather than making them. Relationships help me recognize that on a fundamental level we are connected. I suppose the miracle of discovering the connectedness is most apparent when I start out with the assumption that we are different. Living the human connection with people of another race or culture is a special experience because it moves me past the external differences and touches the fact that we are all made in the image of God. The same holds true for ecumenical sharing. I relate closely to Christians from a variety of denominations. A friend commented that when we live out our traditions fully and deeply, we reach the same deep river of God, the Source that sustains us all. I appreciate that image whether I'm thinking about my religious affiliation or my culture. Mutuality and connectedness don't come from denying the differences but in living them deeply so that we touch the common core at the center of our being. Culture and tradition are external ways of expressing common truths.

Paul's words to the Corinthians teach me how to deal with diversity. He points out that there are varieties of gifts, varieties of services, and varieties of activities. But he always makes the connection back to the common source. It is the same Spirit, the same Lord, the same God. Paul uses the phrase "the same Spirit" four times in four verses! And in case the Corinthians still didn't get the point he repeats the last time, "All these are activated by one and the same Spirit."

I feel challenged to enter into diversity with an attitude of openness to discovering the "same Spirit." I don't gloss over the differences or deny them but move through them to experience the connection.

I wonder how the Spirit has moved in your life to help you discover the innate reality of our connectedness to each other. How have you experienced the "same Spirit" through another culture or faith?

# Life Framed By Death

*Lord, let me know my end, and what is the measure of my days; let me know how fleeting my life is.*
—*Psalm 39:4*

When I ask, like the psalmist, that God let me know the measure of my days and how fleeting my life, I'm not asking to know what date I will die. Measuring my days teaches me how to live. Death provides a framework for life and time is defined by its passing. Each moment is a gift I either live the instant it is given or lose.

# A Hint
# of Eternity

*A hint of eternity steals through my smallest daily activities and perceptions. I am not alone in my tiredness or sickness or fears, but at one with millions of others from many centuries and it is all part of life.* —Etty Hillesum

AFTER A PRESENTATION I gave about the people in El Salvador, I heard a woman turn to her friend and say emphatically, "I'm going to go home and tell my kids they better start appreciating what they have!" Inwardly I shook my head, imagining the futility of demanding that children be appreciative. Appreciation can't be forced on others, so how is it nourished?

I ponder the question. My first thought is, "I can't appreciate what I take for granted." People who live on the edge of life and death can't even take life for granted. It was true first for my mother as she dealt with terminal illness, then several years later for my father. We recognized life was a precious gift as we faced its fragility.

I'm struck by efforts made in the U.S. to protect us

from the reality of our mortality. Sitting around with a group of friends one evening we each shared our most embarrassing moment. One person was hesitant but we insisted until he gave in.

He was at the graveside service of a friend. Heading toward the people gathering to pray, he didn't realize the grass he stepped on was actually Astro-turf covering the burial vault. He caught himself just as he was about to fall through the artificial covering and suffered only a bruised leg.

There was none of the laughter we shared after others told their stories. Rather, we gasped at the thought of how close he had come to unmasking the carefully manicured attempts to hide the reality of death.

The poor in Latin America have no trappings to hide behind. When someone dies, the women prepare the body while the men dig the grave and the children gather flowers. After the casket is lowered into the grave, each person takes turns shoveling dirt into the hole. Tears flow freely as the first clods hit the wooden casket with a hollow thud. Emotions subside as the hole fills and the reverberating echo of dirt on wood slowly fades.

I can't appreciate life unless I'm willing to face my mortality. Then I see my life within the framework of the big picture. "My life is fragile but Life is not," I wrote, shaken by Ann's unexpected death. God, the Source of Life, is eternal. Facing the reality of death keeps my life in perspective and allows "hints of eternity" to enter the here and now.

What experiences remind you that life, as we know it, is fragile? How does facing death put you in touch with God, the Source of Life?

# Enough
# for Today

*Then the Lord said to Moses, "I am going to rain bread from heaven for you, and each day the people shall go out and gather enough for that day. —Exodus 16:4*

MOMENTS OF AWE come as gifts of grace. I can't make them happen and I can't hang on to them.

Mary and I visited the Grand Canyon. We joined about 150 people at the overlook to watch the sunset. As the evening colors took on a surreal glow, a man jumped up on the stone wall behind us. "Hello!" he shouted. "I'm your man from Kodak and I'm here to make this a more meaningful experience by giving you photography tips." I looked around. Sure enough, everyone except Mary and me had their cameras and videos poised to capture the beauty.

The Kodak man continued. "Initially, the colors will be brightest on the east." A rush of people flocked to the east side of the overlook. Five minutes later, he was back on his perch. "Now," he shouted. "Look to the west." One hundred and fifty people stampeded to the west side. Mary and I looked at each other, frustrated. So much for quietly contemplating the beauty of the sunset! The next morning we got up early and watched the sunrise in prayerful silence and solitude.

The sunset experience stays with me. I wish I could stand apart and be critical of the tourists noisily taking pictures. But I can't. I believe everyone present sensed something special was about to happen. That was why they were intent on capturing it on film. It's a natural human tendency to hang on to special moments in an effort to guarantee their availability to us in the future. The problem is that in trying to guarantee the future, I miss living fully in the present.

I'm sure many people who were there that evening now have beautiful pictures of the sunset. But that's all they will be—pretty pictures. They won't have reminders of an experience of wonder at God's creation because they were so absorbed in capturing the beauty they missed the experience of God.

I think about the children of Israel wandering in the wilderness. Exodus 16 explains that God provided food by sending manna from heaven. The manna fell each morning and they were to gather only what they needed. But some tried to store it and the manna spoiled. How do I try to store up God's provisions? When is it difficult for me to trust that God will provide for my needs one day at a time?

Right now I'm dealing with trusting God to meet my personal needs as I anticipate beginning a new MCC assignment. During times of transition I find myself wishing I were married. At least then I would know who I would live with when I return to Central America! But God reminds me that trying to store up for the future gets in the way of living each moment as a gift of grace. I remember the sunset and am reminded that the best way to prepare for the future is to live the full, abundant life God has for me in the present.

How do you experience the relationship between living life moment by moment and trusting God for the future? When do you find it most difficult to trust that God will meet your needs?

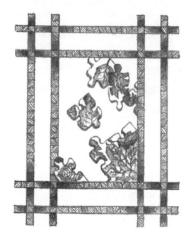

# The "When-Then" Phenomena

*Peace isn't a goal to be reached but a process to be followed. —Leonardo Boff*

I JUST RETURNED from a family gathering. I enjoyed the ten-hour trip and had plenty of time to think about what made it special. The trip was enjoyable because traveling was part of the fun. Sometimes I'm so intent on arriving that I don't enjoy the process of getting there.

The first time I stopped for gas I saw a thrift store so I nosed around the store for a few minutes. When I felt sleepy after lunch I stopped at a rest area and slept for twenty minutes. I saw an art store advertised along the highway and stopped to get some heavy paper for making cards. The stops were spontaneous reminders that I don't have to wait until I arrive at my destination to have fun. I was in such a good mood as I traveled that I didn't even get too frustrated at a road construction traffic jam that delayed me for over an hour. Instead I was grateful that "All Things Considered" had just come on the radio and I had something interesting to listen to as I poked along.

I have to smile as I think about how insignificant it seems to enjoy the trip instead of pushing myself to arrive. But it comes as an important realization that I'm changing in a positive way. I'm not naturally spontaneous. Several years ago I wouldn't even have noticed a thrift store in a strange place, much less stopped. I also tend to be goal oriented. When my eyes are focused on a goal I push myself until I achieve it. In that mind-set, stopping at a thrift store or taking a nap are delays distracting me from my goal.

I'm trying to recall when I began to realize I was missing out on the richness of life by driving myself to meet goals. I remember distinctly sitting in the hammock on our porch in El Salvador trying to explain to a co-worker why I decided not to get involved in a project she thought I should do. I remember exclaiming, "This is my life and I want to live it!" At that point the focus of our discussion changed, and she asked me to explain what I meant.

What did I mean? The civil war had just ended and I was realizing that we were all still functioning under the crisis mentality. The crisis mentality kept us all sacrificing for the "cause," digging deeper and deeper into depleted energy reserves because we were ever so close to achieving our goal. But I was already realizing that the political process was betraying its rhetoric of struggling to bring about justice for the poor. The revolution wasn't living up to its own principles.

By the time the war ended, I was more committed

than ever to nonviolence. The end does not justify the means. The end is determined by the path I take to get there. Leonardo Boff, a Brazilian theologian, said it well when he wrote, "Peace isn't a goal to be reached but a process to be followed." I only arrive at peace by a peaceful path.

It's fine in theory to believe that the end doesn't justify the means. But I've been surprised to realize how deeply the concept of sacrificing to reach goals is ingrained. I saw it in myself and others during the term I studied at seminary. We would sacrifice time alone with God or time spent with people we loved because of studies. The justification was that once the term was over we would nurture the relationships we knew were important. All too often the term ends and other things are pressing. The justification continues. "Once the year ends, then. . . . Once I graduate from seminary. . . . Once I adjust to my new job. . . ."

I've started to refer to it as the "when-then phenomena." My current temptation is, "When I finish writing this book, then I will. . . ." I have to constantly be aware of the "when-then" mind-set, because it creeps in so subtly. It destroys my ability to enjoy living in the present by holding out one elusive goal after another. The goals are like mirages. As soon as I arrive at one it loses its attraction, and I see another looming in front of me demanding that I sacrifice all to achieve it.

When I exclaimed to my friend back in El Salvador, "This is my life. I want to live it," I was listening to the Spirit within me crying out for health and wholeness. The Spirit urges me to be faithful to the process, leaving the results to God.

How have you experienced the "when-then" mindset? How does pushing yourself to reach goals affect your ability to enjoy life in the present? Enjoying the trip to a family gathering gave me reason to celebrate. What small steps along the way give you reason to celebrate?

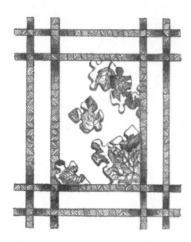

# When Does Life Begin?

*He said to his disciples, "Therefore I tell you, do not worry about your life, what you will eat, or about your body, what you will wear." —Luke 12:22*

I'VE BEEN STRUCK by how many people I've talked to feel stressed and harried. The pressure to achieve is intense and begins early in life. I visited with several youth groups. One urban group was particularly articulate in expressing the stress they feel.

I started out the meeting by explaining that youth in El Salvador are essential community members. The youth are the ones asked by the community to be volunteer health workers or teachers. They have the energy to attend workshops without family responsibilities of their own. The youth are more apt to be able to read and write than the adults. Youth in El Salvador are needed and respected.

"Do you feel needed and respected?" I asked the fifteen or twenty teenagers gathered on the floor. There was silence for a moment before one youth replied, "We're nobodies until we go to college and get a good job."

"Adults don't know what to do with us. We're in the way," another added.

They spoke of the pressure they felt to get good grades to go to a good college to get a good job. "It starts already in elementary school," one explained. A ninth-grader said she was urged to attend a meeting giving tips on getting into college. "It was my first week of high school!" she exclaimed. "I wasn't even adjusted to high school and I was already being told to get ready for college."

"You still haven't 'arrived' when you finish college and find a job," their adviser warned them. "After you get a job, you get married, buy a house, have children, save money to put your children through college. . . ."

I felt compassion as I listened. "When does life begin?" I wondered to myself. No wonder so many teenagers end up in gangs or get in trouble. There is little respect for the gifts they offer at this stage of their lives, only pressure for them to "make something" of themselves.

I also felt sad. I've seen youth materials that essentially advised churches to compete with society by offering youth programs that are exciting and dynamic. But the teenagers I spent time with didn't need to be entertained. They needed to be taken seriously.

How would you answer my question, "When does life begin?" What does it mean for churches to take youth seriously, not as a problem but as gifted members of the community?

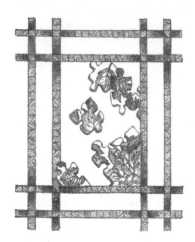

# Puzzle Pieces and Alfalfa Flowers

*When I look at your heavens, the work of your fingers, the moon and the stars that you have established; what are human beings that you are mindful of them, mortals that you care for them? —Psalm 8:3-4*

IT HAS BECOME a family tradition to put together jigsaw puzzles at our Thanksgiving gathering. This year we had a hard one with autumn leaves. When I first sat down to work on the puzzle I was overwhelmed. The pieces seemed indistinguishable. As I concentrated on the tiny pieces, however, I began to notice their minute differences. The shading was slightly different on some. Others had subtly distinct markings. I was amazed that with determined persistence and close attention to detail, we were able to finish the puzzle. A tiny piece, insignificant in itself, left a gaping hole when it was missing. Fortunately we found it on the floor and our puzzle was complete!

An experience last summer also reminded me of the

interplay between small details and the big picture.

I was walking along a country lane when I spotted a tiny purple flower. I walked several more feet searching the edges of the road for another. Then I lifted my eyes and saw a whole field of dainty purple flowers. I knew immediately that I had picked a sprig of alfalfa! When my eyes were narrowly focused on the side of the road, I found the flower. But I didn't know what it was until I saw it within the broader context of the field.

The present moment is like a tiny puzzle piece or intricate alfalfa flower that make up the broad context of my life. Each moment is insignificant in itself but my past is made up of what was the present. And my future is shaped by how I live the details of today. If I pay attention only to each little piece, I get lost in the detail. If I pay attention only to the finished picture, I can't see the pieces that compose it. It isn't one or the other but the constant interplay between both details and context that helps me maintain perspective.

Along with the psalmist, I contemplate the splendor of creation and recognize myself as small and insignificant in comparison. I rejoice that God has mastered the fine art of minute details and global pictures. God not only loves every person but cares about every detail of every person! And God is the Alpha and the Omega, the Beginning and the End, who maintains the tension between the past, present, and future. I have much to celebrate!

How do you maintain perspective between the nitty-gritty demands of daily life and the broad values that give life meaning?

# A Cloud
# of Witnesses

*Therefore, since we are surrounded by so great a cloud
of witnesses, let us also lay aside every weight and the
sin that clings so closely, and let us run with persever-
ance the race that is set before us. —Hebrews 12:1*

YESTERDAY was my mother's birthday and I celebrated
by making hamburgers and french fries. My mother died
in 1981 and would have been seventy-four this year.

It has taken years to learn to honor the memories of
those I love and Central Americans have helped teach
me. I didn't visit my mother's grave until my father died
nine years later and was buried beside her. Central
Americans faithfully visit at least once a year. They in-
vite friends and relatives to pray with them on the first
year anniversary of a loved one's death and continue to
commemorate the death anniversary from time to time.

After my mother died I couldn't understand why I
would feel vaguely depressed around the anniversary of
her death. I didn't yet realize that the cycles and rhythms

of my life will always include September 5, 1981, as a critical juncture whether I'm conscious of it or not. By the time my father died, I had lived in Latin America long enough to want to visit his grave, to want to set aside the anniversary of his death as a special day to pray and remember, to accept that pain would begin to resurface as the anniversary approached.

Honoring the memories of loss doesn't take away the pain but reweaves it into my life with a gentleness absent in the initial shock. Commemorating death anniversaries isn't a morbid act stuck in the past. It's a remembering that creates space for the spirits of those I love to influence me in the present and future. Mary once pointed out that remembering is "re-membering." It knits the severed pieces of our fragmented lives together again.

Anniversaries get easier with time although grief consistently rejects efforts to program or control it. I develop my own little traditions and ways of remembering. On the anniversary of my friend Ann's death, I remember her with a donut and cup of coffee since that was one of her favorite treats when she went to the city for a break.

Friends have also helped me recognize that the spirits of those who have died remain with me. Last year I put together a tool box for myself with some of my father's basic carpentry tools. I thoroughly enjoyed puttering and commented to a friend, "My father would be happy to know I'm using his tools."

She looked at me inquisitively. "What do you mean, 'he *would* be happy?' Don't you believe his spirit lives on? He *is* happy."

It's true. If I believe in eternal life and that the spirit lives on, then I can take comfort in the ways those I love remain present with me. I'm surrounded by a "cloud of witnesses" made up of people who provided faithful examples through their lives and whose spirits continue to enable me to "run the race with perseverance."

My father's birthday is next week. I wonder how I'll celebrate.

I wonder how you are affected by death anniversaries or anniversaries of other significant losses. How can you honor the memories of loved ones who have died?

# Reweaving
# Memories

*All the ends of the earth shall remember and turn
to the Lord; and all the families of the nations shall
worship before him. — Psalm 22:27*

REMEMBERING IS a creative, ongoing process. The psalm-
ist invites me to "remember and turn to the Lord." In re-
membering I don't flee into the past; I create the present.

A number of years ago I was riding in the car with my
mother and a friend of hers since childhood. They were
reminiscing about different events. It didn't take long to
notice a pattern. My mother would remember an expe-
rience recalling the love and joy. Her friend would re-
member the negative side of the same experience.

The circumstances of our lives become the way we
remember them. The memory of an event is woven into
who I am today and the way I remember it affects me
as deeply as the event itself.

I returned to the U.S. when it was clear that Ann's
death was imminent. I spent several days with her, then

went to the motherhouse of the Catholic community to which she belonged. The phone call informing me of her death came in the middle of the Sunday morning church service. I took the call and went back into the church. My memories of that painful experience are enfolded in the love and support I felt from the sisters around me.

Another painful experience comes to mind. Soon after my father died of a brain tumor, the Salvadoran civil war intensified in the area where I lived. I was harsh with myself during those months. I pushed myself hard, compared my pain with the intense suffering of those around me, and was unable to affirm the unpredictable cycles of my grief. It has taken years to allow gentle acceptance to soften those harsh, cutting memories. I was unable to accept my limitations then but now I look back with a sense of humble compassion for the tremendous effort I made to cope in the only way I could at the time.

Healing was hard work. My tendency was to bury the pain. I had to allow the feelings to surface. I had to embrace the feelings with kindness again and again for the memories to soften. Once they softened they could be woven into my life with love instead of harshness.

Other memories well up with joy. Mary and I enjoy reminiscing and share many life-giving memories. We no longer live together and won't live in the same country for the foreseeable future, but the simple memories of moments well-lived continue to nurture us in the present. As Mary pointed out one day, there is nothing left unsaid between us. When one of us dies, the other can take comfort in knowing that the time we spent together was lived fully and deeply. What a blessing!

How have memories shaped your life? I wonder if you have painful memories that need to be gently re-weaved into your life story.

# What Time Is It?

*For everything there is a season, and a time for every matter under heaven: a time to be born, and a time to die; a time to plant, and a time to pluck up what is planted.* —*Ecclesiastes 3:1-2*

ONE COMPLAINT surfaces over and over in North America —lack of time. Almost everyone I visited as I traveled felt pressed for time. Why is that? I wonder as I compare our lives with the lives of friends in rural El Salvador.

Our homes are full of time-saving devices. We have washing machines, stoves, microwaves, cars, refrigerators. The list goes on and on. My Salvadoran neighbors had none of those conveniences yet rarely complained of not having time and consistently took time for relationships. What happens to the time technology frees for us?

Salvadoran peasants have few options for leisure. The young men play soccer on Sunday afternoon and the young women occasionally play softball or embroider.

Adults visit each other. There are special village celebrations several times a year. Life consists of working and spending time with friends or relatives. There are no vacations to plan, hobbies to pursue, televisions to watch, pianos to practice. It's a different story in North America, where we are bombarded with options for how to use our time. Not only each family but each family member faces many possibilities and high expectations for using available time. Even vacations can be filled with trying to take advantage of every opportunity. The saying "too many pots on the fire" is apt as we juggle our way through options and expectations.

During the six months I spent praying and reflecting, I was amazed to discover how deeply I've internalized "busyness." I began those months with a list of things to do. I would respond to all the letters waiting for answers, read the books stacked up unread, pray for all the people I hadn't had time to pray for, and on and on. I felt pressured! How would I get it all done?

Finally I had to stop and laugh. No one, absolutely no one, expected anything of me. If I felt pressure it was because I was pressuring myself. What a relief to laugh at myself, lay my agenda aside, then lay it aside again and again. Yes, there are times stress comes from outside demands but I have been taken aback to discover how much the pressure I deal with comes from within.

I feel challenged to understand time in the biblical sense of season instead of schedule. Knowing the time for the Hebrews wasn't a matter of looking at a watch. To know the time was to trust that there is "a season, and a time for every matter under heaven: a time to be born, and a time to die. . ." (Eccles. 3:1-2). In the Hebrew sense, time isn't an enemy to be mastered but a friend to be discerned.

Sometimes I find myself in a power struggle with time trying to prove I can do it all even as the minutes tick by. But instead of uselessly trying to prove I'm in control, I need to stop and ask, "What time is it?" What is the intended purpose of this moment? Then I become better able to do one task at a time, live one day at a time, enjoy each moment as it comes. I learn to live even in the midst of conflicting demands.

How is your spirit affected by feeling pushed for time? What can you do to get in touch with the intended purpose for this particular season of your life?

# Time-Savers

*The grass withers, the flower fades, when the breath*
*of the LORD blows upon it; surely the people are grass.*
*The grass withers, the flower fades; but the word*
*of our God will stand forever. —Isaiah 40:7-8*

FOR THE PAST two years I've helped a friend who runs a retreat center stuff and address envelopes for the yearly mailing. As I was stuffing envelopes, I was thinking that technology now offers the option of doing the whole process mechanically. The initial investment would pay for itself in several years. Time and money would be saved over the long run.

"Let's listen to the Messiah," Danielle suggested, interrupting my thoughts. We worked peacefully together, sometimes talking, sometimes silent as the music played quietly in the background. An offer of a Snickers bar at the halfway point kept us going! Then there was the promise of supper and the fun of watching a video.

I thought about what I would miss if Danielle had a

machine to do her mailing. Working together is fun. Since many of the tasks I do don't provide measurable results, I enjoyed the satisfaction of looking back and seeing the seven hundred letters we prepared! Yes, the machine would be more efficient—but efficiency doesn't take into account the relationships built as we work at a common task.

The MCC volunteers who now live in the village where I once lived tell me electricity has arrived. People are buying televisions and refrigerators. I wonder how electricity will change their lives. How will TV influence them? Without refrigeration food spoiled quickly. Christmas tamales were made, eaten in great quantities, and shared. Will the generous sharing taper off now that refrigerators allow keeping food for oneself?

Last night on the radio, I heard a report on computers. Businesses all over the world have been computerized. Are they faster and more efficient than before? Hard to measure, the report stated. But business letters, for example, are more expensive now than in the typewriter era. Then a business letter was written in rough draft, then typed in final form. Now business letters go through an average of six revisions before printing. Why? Because in the computer era we expect nearly perfect letters of each other.

A friend in El Salvador went on vacation for a month and left Mary and me his jeep. I was pleased at the thought of a month without the hassle of public transportation. But at the end of the time I gladly returned his vehicle. Easier travel didn't relax my life but increased my expectations of what I hoped to accomplish.

I'm not against technology. In El Salvador I dealt with the contradiction of using a solar panel to run a computer in a village without electricity! But with each new convenience I find it important to ask myself several questions. What am I missing by no longer doing things the old way? The sacrifice often involves relationships.

I also have to ask myself if I'm hoping technology will help me win the battle for time. Am I hoping yet another convenience will let me feel free and relaxed? Then technology is becoming a god. I'm not in control of time and never will be. I must learn to surrender to God who holds the past, present, and future in perspective.

When I feel frantic I hope I can remember to ask, What difference does saving a few minutes here and there make to a God who sees a thousand years like a day (2 Pet. 3:8)? I will only feel free and relaxed when I accept myself as a flower who withers and fades. My purpose in life is to participate in the ongoing work of God which stands forever. Technology may or may not help.

What questions do you ask yourself before you invest in a time-saving convenience? I wonder if you struggle, as I do, with trying to control time.

# Giving Birth

*To surrender all that we are, as we are, to the Spirit
of Love in order that our lives may bear Christ
into the world—that is what we shall be asked.*
*—Caryll Houselander*

To LIVE LIFE FULLY and abundantly I need to recognize
the parameters of mortality. But abundant living also in-
volves recognizing that God is a God of life and I share
in God's fertility. I, along with other celibates, women
who can't have children, or men, have never experi-
enced the biological process of bearing a child. But we
are all called to be fertile.

Meister Eckhart was a fourteenth-century German
theologian who wrote, "The seed of God is in us. . . .
Now the seed of a pear tree grows into a pear tree; and
a hazel seed grows into a hazel tree; the seed of God
grows into God."[11] I think about the parallels between
pregnancy and bringing the seed of God to birth.

During the first trimester, pregnancy is a private, internal process. Some newly pregnant women are confused by the vague symptoms of feeling tired, emotionally vulnerable, and slightly nauseous. There are few outward signs of the tremendous changes that are taking place in her body which makes it difficult to accept the great need to sleep! In Latin America, traditional midwives don't need laboratory tests to confirm that a woman is pregnant because they recognize the early signs. The spiritual birthing of God within me also begins with vague symptoms. I'm more apt to become frustrated with the first signs of new life than to recognize that the seed of God is gestating within me! When I'm experiencing transition or dealing with internal issues, I need a great deal of sleep. Sometimes I feel impatient with myself for feeling tired and depleted. I often feel vulnerable and unable to articulate why. It's then that I'm thankful for spiritual "midwives," friends with wisdom and experience, who encourage me to listen to the obscure signs of change.

There tends to be a certain turning inward during pregnancy. A woman's body must concentrate its resources on nourishing the life growing within. I also experience cycles in my spiritual life when I need to focus my energy inwardly. Since putting my faith into action is important to me, I have to be intentional about not rushing the periods of inward focus. Giving attention to the mystery of life in my soul isn't an escape from outward reality but the only way of assuring that I give birth to Christ in my actions rather than to my own ideas, needs, and ego.

By the time a woman is in the final stages of pregnancy, it's quite apparent that she is about to give birth. I remember going to a Salvadoran market with an MCC volunteer who was nine months pregnant. Pregnancy crosses all cultural boundaries and draws women together. The market vendors freely shared their advice and opinions as to whether my friend was about to give birth to a girl or a boy!

As it becomes apparent that Christ is taking form in a new way within me, I'm better able to talk about that new life with others. I enter into dialogue with people who have also experienced the variety of ways that Christ is born over and over again in our lives. I experience communion with them as we share together. They influence and shape the new life and growth.

How do you bring the seed of God to birth? I wonder how those who have experienced pregnancy see the parallels between being pregnant with a child and the spiritual process of bringing Christ to birth.

# Nibbling
# and
# Gobbling

*For the Lord will not forsake his people; he will*
*not abandon his heritage; for justice will return*
*to the righteous, and all the upright in heart will*
*follow it. — Psalm 94:14-15*

A CARTOON IN a college newspaper depicted the delights
and hazards of spring. A robin finds a worm and has it
clenched in her beak as she pulls it from the ground.
The robin is obviously pleased but as the worm is
stretched toward impending death, it says, "Spring is the
pits." I never thought about spring from a worm's per-
spective!

I wonder what nature was like before the Fall. Did life
for some always depend on death for others? I suppose
I will never know, but it is clear at this point that life de-
pends on death. Annie Dillard points out that nature re-
lies on "nibbling" and being "nibbled upon." A Chinese
proverb expresses it well. "Big fish eat little fish. Little
fish eat bugs. Bugs eat worms." Nature demonstrates a

relationship of give and take.

Certainly at times in my life I've needed to nibble on other people. I'm grateful for friends who willingly nourished and sustained me when I was needy and dependent. I look back now and recognize that sometimes I was relying on others without realizing it. It's hard to accept the help I need in a society where self-sufficiency is valued. At other points, I've allowed myself to be nibbled upon.

"Nibbling" and "nibbling upon" are natural and healthy. The problem comes when we begin to gobble! Some take more than their share of the resources. No longer satisfied with cutting only the wood needed to survive, logging companies bent on profit are destroying the rain forest at the rate of fifty acres per minute. The UN reports that the gap between rich and poor has more than doubled in the past thirty years.

In the short run it looks as if the "gobblers" are winning. I sometimes feel like complaining along with the psalmist, "O Lord, how long shall the wicked, how long shall the wicked exult?" (Ps. 94:3). I need to remind myself that the relationship of cause and effect isn't always readily apparent but justice will prevail. Then I can affirm as the psalmist does several verses later that "the Lord will not forsake his people" (Ps. 94:14).

I wonder what experiences you've had in nibbling on others. When have you allowed others to nibble on you? How do you deal with the fact that some gobble more than their share while others struggle to survive?

# Hope
# Wrapped
# in Struggle

Hope isn't an innate gift
that some have and
others don't. It's nurtured
as we strive to embody
God's love in the midst
of overwhelming
obstacles. Hope
energizes patient
endurance and invites
me to celebrate the
seeds of God's kingdom
taking root.

# Hard-Earned Fruit

*The kingdom of God is not coming with things that*
*can be observed; nor will they say, "Look, here it is!"*
*or "There it is!" For, in fact, the kingdom of God is*
*among you. —Luke 17:20-21*

I OFTEN FEEL helpless when I listen to the news on the radio or watch it on TV. The TV screen is filled with graphic images of suffering and violence. Stories jump from one part of the world to another reporting fragments of compelling events isolated from ongoing relationships with people. The exciting "breaking story" one day is history the next. There is no follow-up or ongoing coverage. It's tempting to bury my head in the sand.

During the past year, I've been observing advertisements. Do advertisements shape our values or reflect them? I suppose it's some of both but anxiety about the future is a key theme. The other day I saw an advertisement for an agenda planner geared to three-year-olds. It was made of vinyl and had colored icons to stick on to help the child remember activities like eating, napping, and playing. According to the instructions, the day planner "helps to alleviate anxiety" and "enhances feelings of importance." What does the concern that three-year-olds are anxious about their schedules say about us?

An ad for health insurance in *Newsweek* played on the theme "What if. . . ." There was a series of pictures indicating unexpected disasters—an accident, losing a job, an illness, a new baby. Under each picture was the caption "What if. . . ." The idea was that we can guarantee our future security through health insurance.

Magazines, news reports, and newspapers are filled with statistics warning us that crime, domestic violence, poverty, environmental concerns are rising. I hear concerns about schools that no longer meet educational standards, the breakdown of the family, and the failure of government structures to represent the American people.

I remember the first several times I returned to the U.S. from El Salvador. I thought that if I could only make people see how bad things were, I could get them to respond. I emphasized appalling statistics and tragic stories. But I no longer think it's helpful to try to scare people into changing. My sense is that many Americans realize something is wrong but the problems are so big we're overwhelmed. We're tempted to withdraw instead of addressing the issues because we feel hopeless and helpless.

As I search for hope in the midst of it all, I need to remind myself not to run from disillusionment. I struggled intensely with feeling disillusioned after the civil war ended in El Salvador. Promises weren't kept. Hopes which inspired people to make incredible sacrifices during the crisis were dashed. Poor people were worse off after the war than before it started. But my disillusionment helped me recognize which of my hopes had been false. It's painful to allow illusions to be stripped away but necessary if I'm to get in touch with truth. In the stripping process I had to deal with feelings of betrayal, self-doubt, wondering if I had been a "sucker" to hope that the political process would bring about positive change. Eventually I was able to recognize the glimpses of genuine hope that sprout like mustard seeds and work under the surface like yeast.

Jürgen Moltmann prophetically identifies the stripping process for a nation in which about 6 percent of the world's population consume about half the resources. "As long as our future drives other people to despair, as long as our prosperity means poverty for others, as long as our 'growth' destroys nature—anxiety, not hope, will be our daily companion."[12]

Some people avoid being stripped of illusions by never facing reality. They live satisfied with superficial signs of hope that make them feel good about themselves. Others see reality and withdraw into passive cynicism. The challenge I feel is that of recognizing reality and still choosing to hope—choosing to trust Jesus' words that the "kingdom of God is among us," choosing not to run from the disillusionment that reveals where I have been duped into believing false promises, choosing to accept that hope isn't handed to me on a silver platter but is the hard-earned fruit of obediently standing against despair.

I wonder how you have experienced disillusionment. What is your sense of where we as a nation place our hope?

# Appreciation

*I will restore the fortunes of my people Israel, and they shall rebuild the ruined cities and inhabit them; they shall plant vineyards and drink their wine, and they shall make gardens and eat their fruit.* —*Amos 9:14*

STRUGGLE REFINES my hope and deepens my sense of appreciation. Amos points to God's hope for bringing Israel back from exile. God dreams of the time when workers will reap the fruit of their labor. "They will plant vineyards and drink their wine; they will make gardens and eat their fruit."

Amos' words are good news to the Salvadorans who pick coffee beans on large plantations but can only afford to drink a coffee substitute made of toasted corn. He says to them, "You will plant coffee trees and drink real coffee." But his words are also good news to those of us far removed from food production. We have the option of buying real coffee but know nothing of the labor involved in caring for the trees and picking the beans. Our pleasure is diminished in ways we don't realize because the food on grocery shelves is the fruit of labor we take for granted.

Before Ann returned to the U.S. for medical treatment, she gave me a starter branch from one of her rose bushes. I did my best to care for the fragile branch. Once it was rooted I planted it in the ground and tended it carefully. During the dry season when there was no longer water in the faucet, I hauled the water it needed. When chickens found their way through holes in our bamboo fence, I doggedly patched the spaces.

But I couldn't conquer the army ants. Three or four times they stripped my precious plant of all of its leaves. Each time I wondered if it would survive. I rejoiced when I saw new leaves beginning to bud on what looked like a dead, dry stick. I celebrated with joy and appreciation the first buds that blossomed almost a year later.

When I returned to the U.S. for a sabbatical, I was aware that daily life would be relatively free of struggle. I would be tempted to forget such struggles and joys as my rosebush represented.

I knew I would quickly begin to assume that water would come out of the faucet when I turned the handle, that lights would come on at the flick of a switch, that washing machines would be available to me. I was right. Over time I began taking those gifts for granted. But I'm not yet trapped. I know conveniences like running water and electricity have nothing to do with my happiness. I know I can live perfectly well without them. I don't yet assume conveniences are my right.

When I sit down to eat I try to remember to pray for the people who worked to make the food available to me. I think about the farmers, the farm workers, the grocery store clerks, and many others. A grateful heart is a gift of grace, a gift that comes wrapped in struggle because struggle breaks through the greatest obstacle to appreciation—taking things for granted.

What can you do to nurture a deeper sense of appreciation in your life? How do you understand the relationship between appreciation and struggle?

# Accounting
# for Hope

*Always be ready to make your defense to anyone who demands from you an accounting for the hope that is in you; yet do it with gentleness and reverence.*
—*1 Peter 3:15-16*

I WAS LOOKING for signs of hope as I traveled across the U.S. during the past six months. I found many seeds of hope, but they are not glamorous or readily apparent.

One example that comes to mind is particularly meaningful because I initially found it depressing. Mary and I visited Eileen, who has worked for twenty-five years with inner-city housing issues and has now started a small educational program. She was a straightforward woman who minced no words in presenting the frustrating reality of working with welfare mothers who are dependent on the system and have little initiative to change. She was astute in her criticism of government programs.

The program she started allows women the opportunity to study for high school equivalency degrees. Study is combined with counseling, since most of the women don't have the self-confidence to believe their lives are worth trying to change. "People seem to think hope comes first, then we're inspired to work toward change," she told us. "But it isn't that way at all. Hope comes through doing."

Eileen and her co-worker have knocked on over two hundred doors in the neighborhood and so far only one woman has accepted the risk of studying for her high school equivalency degree. "What keeps you going?" I asked, impressed with her commitment. "We're here for the handful of women who genuinely want to change," she responded.

As Mary and I climbed in the car after the visit, I commented, "Well, that was depressing!" But the more I thought about it the more I realized a seed of hope was buried in the overwhelming problems. Eileen was on target with her critical analysis of poverty issues. It's clear politics can't account for her hope! Her hopeful attitude only makes sense in the context of love and commitment.

Eileen is motivated by love, so she doesn't need a large "successful" program to energize her. Love enables her to give herself to the slow, crucial process of helping people believe in themselves, a process too often by-passed by large poverty programs concerned with immediate results. Eileen's long-term vision and commitment allow her patiently to nurture any spark of initiative that remains in the women on her block.

Hopefulness in a bleak situation can only be accounted for by the presence of love and commitment. As I work with people who face overwhelming problems, I pray I will be able to gently and reverently account for hope nurtured by love.

I wonder what problems feel overwhelming to you. What motivates you to continue addressing them?

# Energized
# by Hope

*We also boast in our sufferings, knowing that suffering
produces endurance, and endurance produces
character, and character produces hope, and hope
does not disappoint us, because God's love has been
poured into our hearts through the Holy Spirit that
has been given to us. —Romans 5:3-5*

MARIA AND CARMEN are two Mexican-American women
in El Paso, Texas, who recognize that hope is wrapped
in struggle. They work with an organization called La Mu-
jer Obrera (The Worker Woman).

"There used to be twenty garment industries in El
Paso; now there are only four," they told Mary and me.
"The North American Fair Trade Agreement (NAFTA)
was signed in November 1993 and from December to
May eleven factories closed. Much of the garment indus-
try work has moved to poor countries."

María and Carmen explained the problems women
workers face in El Paso. The large garment industries

now contract their work out to small sweatshops. The sweatshop owners are experts on evading taxes, not paying social security, and ignoring workers' rights. When they become concerned that the law is about to catch up with them they close their shop and reopen elsewhere. Sixteen women went to work as usual one day and found that the factory had moved. The workers asked La Mujer Obrera to help them collect the three weeks of back pay that the owner owed them. María and Carmen organized a publicity campaign and the owner paid up several weeks before our visit!

Hope energizes the struggle for change. I'm reminded of Paul's words in Romans 5. "We also boast in our sufferings, knowing that suffering produces endurance, and endurance produces character, and character produces hope, and hope does not disappoint us, because God's love has been poured into our hearts through the Holy Spirit that has been given to us."

Working for change requires patient perseverance. But patience without the fire of hope smolders into passivity and perseverance can become lifeless drudgery. Hope doesn't disappoint us! Hope infuses energy into patient perseverance by keeping God's dreams for the future alive within us, dreams which faith assures us will someday be fulfilled.

Hope is not innate. It isn't a learned theory. It isn't a gift some have and others don't. Hope is refined by the challenge of making God's dreams visible on earth.

How have you experienced hope? What do you think of the concept that "hope is wrapped in struggle?"

# My Task

*We cannot die on every cross, nor are we expected to . . . [God] working within us, portions out [his] vast concerns into bundles, and lays on each of us our portion.* —*Thomas Kelly*

SHOPPING IS a dilemma for me. Soon after returning from El Salvador, I wanted to buy a pair of slacks. I found some I liked and checked the label, "Made in El Salvador." I immediately put them back. I feel connected to the women in El Salvador who endure poor working conditions and unjust wages as they sew. I can imagine what they look like, where they live, where they work. A tag that says "Made in El Salvador" brings names and faces to my heart.

I went on to the next pair of slacks, "Made in Bangladesh." I don't feel the same connection to people in Bangladesh. It's easier to buy clothing made someplace where I can't picture the faces of people receiving unfair wages. But by that time the inconsistencies and contradictions were too great. I didn't buy anything. Later I ended up buying a pair of slacks at a thrift store. At least clothes there are one step removed from unjust working conditions!

The day after I wrote about María and Carmen I received information in the mail about the working conditions in a garment assembly plant in San Salvador. The workers assemble clothes for U.S. companies. A shirt that costs $20.00 in the U.S. brings a $0.12 earning for the workers, mostly young women, who sew them. Many of the workers are minors. Once or twice a week they are forced to work eighteen hour shifts. Over three hundred workers were fired when they organized to better their working conditions.

Today I wrote a letter to one of the primary U.S. companies contracting work there. I know one letter won't make an impact. If thousands of people wrote, the company would probably change, not due to values or principles but out of concern for sales. But I doubt thousands of people will protest, so what good did it do for me to write?

I wrote because I needed to write, not because I'm convinced my letter will make a difference. I needed to be faithful to the voice within me that declared that the situation was outrageous and unacceptable. Being faithful may or may not bring about the results I want. It's true lots of letters might make an impact, but I have to be careful not to base my actions on what others decide. I can't sit back until I'm convinced enough people are writing to make the endeavor "successful" according to my definition.

Thomas Kelly, a Quaker, wrote, "The loving Presence does not burden us equally with all things, but considerately puts upon each of us just a few central tasks, as emphatic responsibilities. . . . We cannot die on every cross, nor are we expected to. . . . [God] working within us, portions out [his] vast concerns into bundles, and lays on each of us our portion. These become our tasks."[13]

Kelly's words are a challenge to all of us. My tendency is to pick up more than my share of the bundles. The challenge for me is to carry only what God asks without taking responsibility for bundles left untouched. Perhaps some people tend not to pick up their share of the bundles. The challenge for them is to accept the tasks God asks of them.

God asks me to be faithful to my tasks. I'm most effective when I faithfully carry my bundle. I might not see the fruits or the results I wish. But I can trust that I'm contributing to an ongoing process that is broader than my gifts and beyond my lifetime.

How do you deal with the tension between being faithful and being effective? Do you tend to try to carry more than your share of God's "bundles" or are you one who needs to be prodded to pick up your share?

# Embodying Dreams

*God's kingdom is not something we build. God's kingdom has always been there. When we are converted we become aware of it, we begin to see its signs and we set about to embody it so that others, too, can see it and take hope. — Walter Klaassen*

DREAMING IS a long-term investment in the future. Last year a friend planted a small plot of ginseng root in the woods. Ginseng, a medicinal plant, is a lucrative crop which requires little investment of money or time. But there is one drawback. It takes ten years to produce!

Dagoberto, a Salvadoran from a rural peasant family, was sixteen when I met him. He was a local health worker who dreamed of becoming a doctor. Since there was no high school in his small town, he studied by correspondence. His dream continues to motivate him, and Dagoberto is now in his second year of university. When the funding he was promised fell through, a woman who believed in his dream committed herself to finance his schooling.

It's a risk to support long-term dreams. Dagoberto might not be able to make it through medical school and his commitment to help the poor might be corrupted by the influences around him. But on the other hand, this talented, determined young man might remain faithful to his call to dedicate himself to his people. One woman with the financial means to support him is willing to sacrifice immediate gratification and quick payback to risk investing in the kind of dream that makes the kingdom of God visible. My heart wells up with gratitude for her.

We can't control when and how dreams are fulfilled. Larry is an avid gardener who lives in Denver. When he and his family moved to a new house, he noticed an empty lot beside them. Why not start a community garden? Larry tracked down the owner. She was an elderly woman who bought the land forty-five years before hoping to use it someday as a community garden!

I need to be aware of my tendency to try to make dreams come true or to take on myself the responsibility of building the kingdom of God. I was challenged by Walter Klaassen's reminder that we are to "embody" God's kingdom which is already here among us. Building it is God's responsibility!

It's humbling to think that we make God's dreams visible, but surely Dagoberto embodies God's dream for a world where everyone has access to health care. The woman financing his schooling embodies God's dream for a world in which people support and enable each other. Larry embodies God's dream for neighbors who constructively work together.

God plants within us dreams that coincide with God's hope for the future. Those are the dreams I know will bear fruit someday.

Who are the people in your life who embody the kingdom of God? I wonder how you deal with the tension between long-term dreams and the need to see results. I'm also curious about how you understand the difference between building the kingdom of God and embodying it.

# Repetition

*I will instruct you and teach you the way you should*
*go; I will counsel you with my eye upon you.*
*—Psalm 32:8*

I SPENT SEVERAL HOURS this afternoon loading a wheelbarrow full of split wood to fill the woodshed. Back and forth, back and forth. Load and unload. I gradually entered into the repetition. It felt good to use my body after sitting at the computer most of the morning. I also enjoyed working on a concrete task that provided a sense of immediate gratification. After several hours I could see that we had moved enough wood to fill the shed!

I thought about repetition. Does it have negative connotations, like "ordinary"? I've been concerned because much of what I'm writing seems repetitious. The same themes come out over and over again in different ways. But that's the way I learn. Maybe I don't need to apologize for the repetition or cut it out of the final manuscript. God evidently doesn't tire of repeating because

the same lessons come up time after time!
I'm sensing that the same issues will repeat themselves throughout life because they are *my* issues. They will be with me always. I don't need to be harsh with myself, thinking that surely I should have learned that lesson by now. Hopefully I will learn to laugh gently and humbly. Yes, I will always need to be reminded to trust my heart as well as my head. Yes, I will always need to be challenged to surrender control. Yes, I need to remember to live in the present and not worry about the future. Those are my issues. Change will come as I befriend them and stop trying to conquer them once and for all.

Hope inspires me as I learn and forget and learn again. Hope doesn't judge my progress by measuring it against perfection. Rather, it invites, encourages, and draws me toward the love and patience I need in order to learn. Hope keeps patience energized so I neither become complacent nor give up in despair.

Last year the theme of living in the present was important to me. I thought I had new insights that would change my tendency to want to control the future. But one afternoon I found in my Bolivia journal a page of quotes that had to do with living the present. Twelve years before I was already being drawn to live more fully in the present. So much for new insights!

I am grateful that God is a patient teacher familiar with my need to keep learning and relearning the same lessons in different ways. I'm thankful that "God's eye is upon me" and that God "gives me counsel." I pray for the ability to humbly befriend my need for repetition.

I shared some of the issues that keep coming up in my life. What issues do you come back to over and over again? As you finish this book perhaps you can think of ways to continue working with them.

# Notes

1. John Kavanaugh, "Imperceptible Life, Incomprehensible Death," *America*, June 4-11, 1994.
2. Henri Nouwen, "Power, Powerlessness, and Power," *Weavings*, Jan./Feb., 1995, p. 38.
3. Robert D. Cornwall, "The Way of the Cross: The Anabaptist Concept of 'Gelassenheit,' " *Studia Biblica et Theologica*, Vol. 17. 1:33-53, April 1989, p. 33.
4. Gerald G. May, *Will and Spirit* (San Francisco: Harper & Row, 1982) p. vi.
5. Nouwen, pp. 36, 38.
6. Klassen, William, *Covenant and Community: The Life, Writings and Hermeneutics of Pilgram Marpeck* (Grand Rapids, Mich.: Eerdmans, 1968), p. 56.
7. Robert A. Johnson, *Owning Your Own Shadow* (San Francisco: Harper & Row, 1991), p. 7.
8. Gerald G. May, *The Awakened Heart* (San Francisco: Harper & Row, 1991), p. 16.
9. Henri Nouwen, *The Living Reminder, Service and Prayer in Memory of Jesus Christ* (San Francisco: Harper & Row, 1984), p. 28.
10. Jack Nelson-Pallmeyer. *War Against the Poor, Low-Intensity Conflict and Christian Faith* (Maryknoll, N.Y.: Orbis Books, 1989), p. 10.
11. Matthew Fox, *Meditations with Meister Eckhart* (Santa Fe, N.M.: Bear and Co., 1983), p. 28.
12. Jürgen Moltmann, *Experiences of God* (Philadelphia: Fortress Press, 1980), p. 24.
13. Thomas Kelly, *A Testament of Devotion* (New York, N.Y.: Walker & Co., 1987), pp. 108, 123.

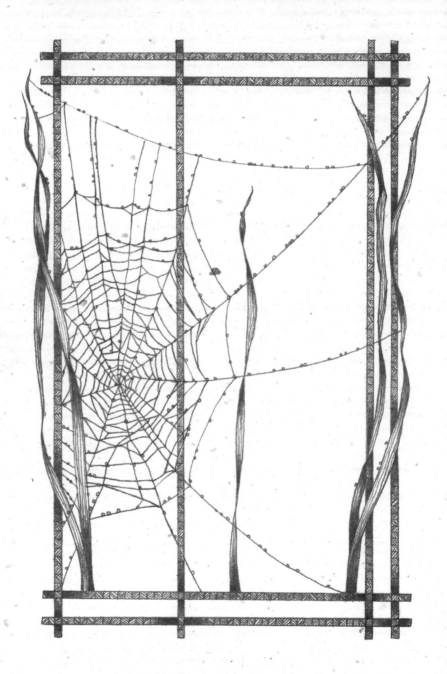